A Collection of Old Men

A Collection of Old Men

Judy Sutcliffe

Seven Gables Press
Mineral Point, Wisconsin
2010

ISBN: 978-0-692-00679-5

Seven Gables Press
PO Box 42
Mineral Point, WI 53565
www.sevengablespress.com
electype@netexpress.net

The Bee Man *and* Old Dogs *were first published in*
Frank Beaman's Mineral Point Times.

Other books by Judy Sutcliffe:
Iowa Lyric: Poems of the Changing Seasons
Grandma Cherry's Spoon: A Story of Tuberculosis

Books are available from
Longbranch Gallery, Mineral Point, Wisconsin
info@longbranchgallery.com 608-987-4499

Table of Contents

Preface

The small stories gathered here are ninety-nine percent true. Sometimes I'm a little fuzzy about dates and the passing of time. The quotes I've written down are not verbatim, as I wasn't carrying a tape recorder. But they are close to what was said. Sometimes I leave a few details out, but you won't know that. I may have changed a few names here and there. Otherwise, the various gentlemen gathered here are true, real, and mostly dead.

But I remember them very much alive.

The stories hop around a bit. No particular order. Jump in anywhere. To give you a little framework, here's where I was during the times and events recounted:

1941 born in Hays, Kansas
1945-59 Audubon, Iowa
1959-63 University of Iowa, Iowa City
1963-1967 Old Town, Chicago
1967-1968 Hagen-Haspe, Germany
1968-1978 Audubon, Iowa
1978-1996 Santa Barbara, California
1996-2000 Audubon, Iowa
2000-present Galena, Illinois, and
       Mineral Point, Wisconsin

Judy Sutcliffe

To
Sandy,
my own age

and no gentleman

I took this photo of Norbert Schiller when he was 82.

The Curtain Falls

IN HIS EARLY EIGHTIES he had chortled to himself in a poem about "taking up hang gliding and other forms of suiciding." I still have the little slip of paper with his tiny, spikey writing.

He enjoyed too much, however, the tiny cups of espresso downtown each day and his wife's thyme-scented vegetarian casseroles at night. He took the bus into downtown Santa Barbara every morning, an aged leather visor clamped over his unruly, Einsteinian hair, a flat leather pouch tucked under his arm.

His shoulders were bent more than he liked. Still, even without the stage that had been his young world, he could manage to procure an audience. He would seat himself on a bench in the sun and wait for a victim to sit beside him. Preferably a young, pretty, female, and impressionable victim.

"Do you like poetry?" he might throw out as his first snare. "Let me read you one that you will like." Too polite to get up and move and mildly intrigued, the girl would nod assent, thinking, "He looks harmless."

Norbert Schiller would then create a little dramatic suspense by slowly opening his leather pouch and appearing to—slowly—examine the slips of paper inside as if in search of the perfect poem for his now-expectant audience. He knew very well what he would read, and he knew it, in fact, by heart. But a little quiet delay, in which the girl might admire his still handsome profile, his momentous moustache, and his shock of silvery hair always helped the effect.

Then he would read his poem, leaning his visor carefully against the sun, and the girl would go into literary shock. His voice, trained in the Vienna State Theater in the 1920s, when he was a starving youth of great natural talent, would cast the words of the poem, any poem, into nuances of sound rarely ever experienced in American theatre. The strong, precise, exquisitely modulated delivery, coming from a frail, bent old man, was so unexpected as to be electrifying.

Young women fell in love with him every day on the streets of Santa Barbara. The magic did not always last beyond a poem or two. Sometimes it got him a cup of espresso in pleasant feminine company, sometimes an opportunity to deliver a genuine, moist, Viennese hand kiss, of which he was an expert practitioner. Sometimes it brought him a repeat rendezvous. Sometimes a friend.

It was what he did with his days as an old man.

And then one morning, outside the small house he

shared with Mary, three decades younger, he fell. If Mary had seen him, she would have helped him up, scolded him, and put a Band-Aid on his elbow. But it was a kindly neighbor who witnessed the fall and, doing the right thing, called 911, the city emergency number.

The circus began with the swift siren call of the emergency truck, the sudden jolting transport to the hospital, the misplacement of his glasses. A fog surrounded him, through which his wife's voice seemed to speak from a distance, reassuring. But he was not reassured at all. Strange white shapes floated in and out of his range of vision, and after a sleepless night, he began to assume they must be angels. Needles and tubes were inserted in assorted orifices, including a catheter, since the angels didn't have leisure to escort him to the bathroom every hour.

Confusion increased, and he pulled the catheter out. The angels then tied his hands to the bed rails and reinserted the catheter. Mary seemed further away and chattered on about needing to stay long enough for Medicare to pay for the hospital bill. He was upset enough one day to tell me that he intended to commit suicide by hanging himself. Since this was a man who did not know how to wield a screwdriver, I wasn't much worried, though I considered his intentions practical, under the current circumstances.

By the time he was taken home, two weeks later, he had lost touch with humans as well as angels and was never quite himself again. No point in getting new glasses at 87. Things remained foggy.

He now lay in his own room, on the narrow, wooden bed which he had slept on for years, with no mattress beneath him, probably thinking it improved his posture. The room was ascetic as a monk's, with a few small, soft leather-bound books—Schiller's works, Jacob Boehme, Goethe, Hölderlin—the classics he had lived with. A few dried quatrefoil sepals from persimmons lay on his desk, and that was about all.

He had not been able to bring much with him when he escaped the Nazi assault on Austria. All that he had was sewn into his heavy greatcoat. He acted his way out of the country as Hitler was entering.

One of the small treasures that survived was a palm-sized spiral notebook he gave to me in a lucid moment. It contained the essence of photos of his lovers, mostly actresses, from his years as a romantic heartthrob on the German stages from Berlin to Munich. Essence was what he loved, the essence of coffee, the essence of beloved women. The pages were adorned with pasted cuttings of photos, one woman's eyes, another's legs. The childlike profile of Helene Mayer, her hair in great blonde coils, Olympic fencer, the most beloved.

Mary's large brown eyes looked out of a gaunt facial structure. She practiced Tai Chi in the backyard in sweat pants and an old undershirt. "I wasn't expecting to be his nursemaid," she said, lunging forward on one small foot. She admired her husband, his distant, golden past, but caretaking was not her forte. She was impatient. Nevertheless, she accepted her temporary fate with only slightly reluctant grace and cooked and cleaned.

Many months later, Hospice entered the scene with a hospital bed, assuming that the curtain would imminently fall for Norbert, now nearly blind and immovable. A hefty neighbor came every day to help turn him and lift him for bathing.

I came to visit occasionally, and one day Mary stared at me and said, her eyes rather wide, "When this is over, I am going to the Australian outback and ride a camel."

"That," I thought, "is why he married her."

The last conversations I had with him were about his dreams. It was harder and harder for him to distinguish night from day, and dreams took over much of his consciousness. He told me he had a recurring dream that he was on a train heading from Austria into Hungary, with the promise of a lead role in a play at his destination.

"But I get off the train before we cross the border," he complained. I suspected that he was still enjoying the fruits of the earth in his wife's cooking. But finally, even the casseroles failed to keep him from his new role.

Mary called me, "I'm afraid to go in his room. I think he's dead. I'm afraid to touch him. Can you come over?"

We stood in the doorway and gazed at him, still sitting half upright in the hospital bed. His eyes were open. His skin had taken on the color of old, yellowed ivory, the best he'd looked in some time, he'd be glad to know, I thought.

"Have you got a mirror?"

Mary produced a hand mirror which I held above Norbert's lips, ala movies and murder mysteries. No discernible moisture breathed forth. I closed his eyelids.

"I suppose we have to call the doctor now," Mary said.

"No, we don't have to just yet. Let's sit down in the kitchen with a pot of tea for awhile first." The afternoon sunlight fell gently on the plates and cups.

A train arrived at the station, and a young man with dark, curling hair and dark-lashed, very blue eyes stepped out and sniffed the fresh breeze. Six months later I received a photo in the mail of Mary on a camel somewhere in the Australian outback.

Norbert Schiller as a young actor.

The Ballroom Dance

THE BAND MEMBERS who played for Saturday night ballroom dances at the Santa Barbara rec center were about as old as their waltzes and foxtrots. But the four septuagenarians never lagged on rhythm or speed. They were pros. And just in case their mostly elderly dance patrons were unsure of how to arrange their feet, they placed a signboard on the stage with markers designating the order of the dances in the set: a polka, a tango, a Viennese waltz, and so forth.

I was probably, in my early fifties, the youngest in the ballroom. And also, perhaps, the most nervous, as I'd never had the courage to come alone to a public dance before. I'd taken plenty of swing dance lessons, but I had not ventured out to a dance by myself. Now I was on my own, and so were almost all the dancers on the floor. Few appeared to have come with partners.

There were, of course, more women than men, and most of them were quite gussied up in flowing gowns, high heels, and considerable make up and hair spray. No matter how ancient, when they whirled and twirled under softly dimmed room lighting, they sparkled from the ever-circling, slightly dizzying dots of light thrown from a mirrored ball that revolved slowly at the center of the high ceiling. They looked like the Dancing Princesses of fairy tales.

I wore a black skirt to my knees, a short-sleeved black overblouse, black dance sandals with a very modest heel height, no jewelry, no make-up, and no hair spray. My long, rather fine, light brown hair was pinned up precariously.

I examined the short supply of males. I had come to the conclusion, after watching several of the actively dancing women, that if I wanted to dance—and I did—I had to do something. I could not sit in the folding chairs on the sidelines and expect my prince to come. I either had to walk up to a prospective partner and boldly, if coquettishly, ask for a dance, or, I had to stand in the main doorway and look charming, eager, and toe-tapping ready.

Some of the male dancers were very good, and the fancy dancing ladies easily snatched them up. I wondered if any of the older gentlemen would deign to spin me around the floor. Although I could follow most basic leads, I didn't know how to do the delicate toe and heel sweeps that many of the dance-schooled women executed in their pointy-toed slippers.

I seriously entertained the thought of sneaking outside and going home. I stood up and nonchalantly worked my way toward the big entry doorway where the ladies were milling around, preening their feathers, and looking for the next partner for the next dance. I could see my escape route to the doors beyond that would open to the front sidewalk.

A man wearing a black Greek fisherman's cap, his back to me, stood amidst the women. The cap surmounted a fine tangle of curling, greying, reddish hair. He wore a black leather vest over a blue shirt, and his knees in black trousers were a bit bowlegged. He seemed quite chipper. He was teasing a couple of the women.

He turned around suddenly, and I met his blue eyes amid freckles, a strong, straight nose, and a grin. He looked friendly. I walked right up to him and said, "Would you like to dance?"

"Oh, would I!" he said and grabbed my hand, pulling me after him onto the floor. A waltz had just started. I figured out in the first three steps that there was no way to dance with this man except by the most intuitive following of his unusual, but very strong, lead. He did not dance by the rules. He danced in perfect rhythm with the music, but he made up his own moves, his own steps and whirls, and he didn't repeat them in any cognizant pattern.

My intuition tuned to total automatic, I followed his every move, his every swirl and dip. Once he had assured himself that I was able to follow him accurately, he swept forward in ever more bizarre and unrepeatable steps. His strong right hand at my waist told me exactly where to go. He was totally controlling in the best sense, and in ballroom dancing, there's little room for equality of decision making. He lead, I followed. I loved it.

After the dance, at midnight, I followed him right outside into a long kiss leaning into a hibiscus bush full of blossoms. And the next day, still a bit dizzy, I drove to Ventura to look for the old sailboat he was working on in the harbor drydock.

Willie Craig on his boat in Ventura Harbor.

The Goldfish

MY FATHER was not adverse to a practical joke now and then.

As a country veterinarian in and around the town of Audubon, Iowa, he soon discovered a considerable waste of his time due to party telephone lines. He would be on a farm at the far reaches of Audubon County. He would finish doctoring the calf or cow or sow or horse—he was a large animal practitioner. He would wash off his instruments and his boots with water he always carried with him in a tall round cream can. Then he would petition the farmer to use their phone to call my mother. He wanted to find out if any emergency calls had come in that were located in that corner of the county. It would save him gas plus wear and tear on his Jeep bouncing around the mud and gravel roads of the early 1950s.

But party lines were life lines to farmers' wives in those days, and they were very frequently occupied, not only by the two parties engaged in lengthy conversation, but also by all the extra ears listening to the best gossip grapevine ever invented.

My father was not very patient. Rather than wait for phone lines, his solution was to purchase his very own phone line, one of the earliest two-way shortwave radio stations in the area. For the antenna he bought a windmill tower from a farmer and set it up right behind our modest house, there being no such thing as architectural reviews in our little town. My sister and I and the neighbor kids were most definitely not allowed to climb it.

A portable shortwave unit with a microphone on curly wire was positioned in the Jeep by Dad's seat, and a base unit operated by my mother took up residence in the laundry room.

The first thing Dad did with that rig was to drive the Jeep a short block away to his favorite auto mechanic. He left the radio turned on.

He walked back to our house and his office and stood in the driveway watching the service bay at the repair shop. My mom and I were hanging around, wondering what was going on. Dad didn't stand still very often.

The moment he saw the Jeep hoisted up in the air and his favorite mechanic reaching up under it, he darted into the house. We followed him and heard him pick up the shortwave microphone. He did not give the call letters—KAC939— that were supposed to always accompany use of the radio. He just started giggling, then laughing, then guffawing. Then he said, in a high-pitched voice, "Oh, stop, stop, you're tickling me!"

And then he quickly hung up the mike and dashed back outside to watch a very befuddled mechanic.

Dad's practical jokes were never malicious or demeaning, just gently humorous, eliciting smiles and devious revenge. And once, at least, he did something that was taken entirely seriously at the time. The smiles and gentle laughter of recognition appeared only many years later.

One summer afternoon Dad was outside our house and his office, watering his abundant vegetable garden, when a small girl walked up to him with a fishbowl in her hands, displaying a belly-up dead goldfish.

"My fish got sick, Doc," she said. "Can you make him well?"

Dad poked the fish gently with his finger. "Maybe," he said. "You leave him here with me and come back in an hour."

An hour later she returned to find her goldfish swimming merrily around in its tiny bowl. "He just needed a little medicine," the veterinarian said.

A middle-aged woman told that goldfish story at my father's memorial service, adding how unfortunate it was that the Dime Store had closed, so we couldn't buy "Doc" Sutcliffe such a quick resurrection.

Norbert Schiller at his former stone house in Ojai, California.

A Meeting

THE PROPRIETOR of Mud Hen Press probably didn't bother the second year, but the first year of the Book Festival in Santa Barbara, she was so heavily inspired she lugged a small black iron printing press to the exhibition hall and put up a sign offering to print small poems, on the spot, for free. Using metal type.

I looked at the samples she had already printed that day, felt the depth of the letters' impressions in the soft, thick paper. I found a pencil in my purse and stood there trying to remember some small poem I had written in the past.

An old man stood not far away, also engrossed in the printed samples. His hair was silvery, unruly, and thick, curbed by a dark leather visor. He was very thin, his shoulders bent a little. He had a large leather envelope tucked under his arm.

I handed the woman my few words and watched as she plucked tiny bits of metal from a typecase. She explained the process to me as she worked. She was setting someone else's poem and would do mine a little later. I wandered about the booths, amazed at how many small publishers had emerged for this auspicious literary occasion.

It was exhilarating.

A poem was published. I picked up the handful of pale green cards with my few words immortalized upon the thick paper in fine, black print. I could feel the words.

I stumbled outside with my treasure and stood in the sunlight filtering through the eucalyptus trees, reading and rereading this magical thing that happens when words and handwriting emerge as print.

"May I see your poem?" said a voice with a German accent. It belonged to the old man with the hair and the leather. He shuffled closer, and it occurred to me that he might be one of the homeless people in the city. His heavyweight corduroy trousers were faded and worn. His shirt had a stain on the front. His feet were bare in scuffed sandals.

I hesitated, my reverie now broken, then handed him one of the pale green cards.

He turned slightly, shading the card with the shadow of his visor.

And then he read aloud my poem with a caressing voice that gave each little word, each syllable, the nuanced, arching grace of meaning that even a printing press could not express. This was not an ordinary voice.

He looked up at me with pale but very blue eyes, with the faintest smile hiding under his moustache. Just then a man and woman came by, greeting Norbert by name and nodding to me. "Let's all go to the Mesa Cafe," they said. The woman looked at me, calculating. "Why don't you bring him," she said.

His name was Norbert Schiller and he was not related to the other Schiller, but he started quoting something grandiose in German as we walked slowly to my little red Volkswagen bug. He was 82. He managed to collapse his knees into the passenger seat, and we took off. He progressed to *Faust*, and told me that Goethe had fallen in love with a 16-year-old girl when he was 82. I was 41, and I drove the wrong way up a one-way street.

G.B. Shaw at Church Camp

THAT JAZZ DANCING body, long brown legs kicking to the side, so exquisitely animal, always with that radiant smile and saucy eyes—Josephine Baker on YouTube, courtesy of her fans who bring snippets of her films to the great web of watchers.

Suddenly I remember Shaw and the Black Girl, and I wonder, did Bernard Shaw ever see Josephine Baker on stage in Paris in the 1920s? She was so well known, such a graphically visual image, revolutionary in all ways. Maybe a long shot, but Josephine could have inspired Shaw's little book, *The Adventures of the Black Girl in Her Search for God,* or at least, his illustrator. The book's woodcuts of a naked black African girl accosting varied delusions of gods have lived long in the back of my mind.

I was a young teenager in Iowa in the 1950s, before the civil rights marches began. One summer I attended a week long Methodist church youth camp at Springbrook Park near Guthrie Center. My attendance was primarily because I had a crush on my local Audubon, Iowa, minister's daughter, not because I felt particularly Methodistical. Being friends with Helen required a few sacrifices like church attendance and this camp.

I took a lot of clothes with me, including a full circle cherry red skirt with a cute bib and suspenders, along with a poofy net underskirt.

And the one person I met and most admired at the camp didn't like red. I didn't quite understand why, but in his native Nigeria, it was not a good color for a woman to wear. To this day I feel uneasy in a red jacket.

His name was Fola, and he was what the camp ministers called a "national," someone from a foreign country who would be spiritually inspiring to impressionable young Methodist boys and girls. They underestimated the depths of impressionability. I fell quickly in love with Fola. He was several years older than me, and either in or just out of college. He spoke English very well, with a softly turning accent that intrigued me. He gazed at me with thoughtful, proud, and saddened eyes.

I had never seen a black human being before, up close, in person. He was very easy, open, and friendly to everyone. I was curious, and, although a little shy, I initiated conversations. I soon found out that he was very knowledgeable about English literature, and that being one of my budding interests, we began to seek each other out to talk about books.

He loved the plays of George Bernard Shaw, especially the philosophic prefaces, and he made me want to run to a library immediately. The Shaw book that he most recommended to me, however, was *The Adventures of the Black Girl in Her Search for God.*

"This is a story about a young native woman in the jungles of Africa," he explained to me. We were sitting at a picnic table in the shade.

"A missionary gives the girl a Bible. She sets out in search of the God of the Bible, but in fact meets a series of gods. This was Shaw's way of showing that the idea of God was depicted in several distinctively different ways through the Old and New Testaments." My eyes followed his gracefully gesturing hands, watching the lightness of his palms and the underside of his fingers.

"She finds none of the gods worth listening to and goes on to meet Voltaire, who advocates that she simply cultivate her garden. In the end she meets a red-haired Englishman who looks suspiciously like Shaw and marries him." He smiled at me with white teeth and no little amusement at my wide-eyed interest.

"She enjoys a happy and fruitful life with her Irishman, with no further need to ask religious or philosophical questions. I'll see if I can find a copy of the book for you," he said. I wanted to touch his hair and his cheek, but did not move.

Shaw's tale didn't sound to me as if it would be on the Methodist, Catholic, or Jewish recommended reading lists. The world of literature was far more expansive than church dogma, I already knew.

"There are things I cannot explain," he said. It was a warm summer day and tiny beads of moisture were forming across the darkness of his brow. "I remember in my village, a group of men around an elder. He drew a circle in the dust. It turned into a snake and slithered away. I saw it myself. There are mysteries that are real."

"I don't understand it, but I can believe it," I said. "I know that my mother saw her father a few days after he died. There's no explanation. My mother doesn't lie."

A tenderness developed between us in those few days. I had never met anyone who had read so many meaningful books and liked to talk about them as if they were important to one's life. We sought each other out whenever there was an opportunity.

The end of the week approached. We would soon disappear into the worlds we had emerged from, with a very slim chance of meeting again. He would be returning to Nigeria in the near future.

The day before the week ended we left the campground together in the early afternoon to walk around Springbrook Lake nearby. I was pleased and mildly embarrassed to be with him. I had never yet had a date with a boy. After passing the swimming beach, we walked slowly along a narrow path, moist and earthen, close to the edge of the small, quiet lake. As we wandered along the ragged way, distant sunlight flickered through the woodland canopy above us, and slim hickory trees, gooseberry bushes, and Virginia creeper crowded around us, right to the edge of the water. We walked carefully along, jumping over muddy spots, not talking very much, and quite alone. Insects buzzed in the air. No one else seemed to be anywhere but at the swimming beach. Their laughing, shouting voices grew softer and softer the further we walked.

A shy anticipation excited my being. We were far away from the rest of the world, and we were alone with each other, and we did not need to speak. We were bathed in the earth's summer warmth, brushing our skins against the leaves that leaned into the path. It narrowed the further around the lake we walked. The trees seemed taller, the path ahead more shadowy. Our pace slowed, and now and again we stopped to admire a wildflower.

But eventually we saw in the distance sunny fields and the grass-covered dam. We'd reached the end. We paused, reluctant to leave the shadowed greens of the forest just yet. We sat down on a patch of grass within the pleasant shade of a tall tree. We were both shy and full of effervescing feelings. I found myself gazing deeply into his large, dark eyes or lowering my glance to the grasses.

"Why is the skin of your cheeks so pink?" he asked, and I had no answer. I watched, as he talked, his gesturing hands, with their strange and lovely pink inner palms. We talked ourselves into silence. He reached across it, looking into my eyes, and with one gentle finger, he touched my right upper arm, drawing his slim fingertip lightly down my pale skin.

That was all. It was almost more than either of us could bear.

We walked slowly back to the camp to find the several ministers waiting and watching. Perhaps we had been gone too long. To their credit, they didn't say anything, but it was obvious to Fola and me that they were making sure all the next day that we were never alone together again. If we started to speak to each other, a counselor would quickly approach and start up a pleasant conversation.

We managed, however, to exchange addresses, and letters passed between us in months following. He sent me a copy of Shaw's *Black Girl,* with the beautiful woodcuts of the naked young woman, so like Josephine Baker in supple beauty and total self-confidence. I sent for a Modern Library edition of Shaw's plays and read all the prefaces. I was a socialist for at least six months.

I dreamed one time of Fola and of a tall chain link fence between us. I'm not sure which of us was imprisoned. I only recall his sadness and his strange gesture of putting two fingers through the fence, which I took into my mouth. The Presbyterian minister and the daughter of our high school principal went south to join the civil rights marches.

Fola returned to Nigeria, and I lost track of him.

Until the Google Era. And then I found him, in Oregon, teaching in a college there. He has a wife and grown children. And white hair. But his memory of that week in the Iowa woods matches mine.

Over the Fence

DOORBELL rang amid pounding and an excited woman's voice. I opened the door to my small neighbor lady, tendrils of black hair flying amid agitated hands and a torrent of Spanish that I didn't understand, except for one word, telefono. She was weeping.

I didn't know her name and had only smiled at her across our mutual Santa Barbara neighborly fence a few times as she was pushing her children out the gate and off to school in the mornings. Her husband was a car salesman in a suit and was comfortably bilingual, as were the children.

It was her father that I particularly liked. He would walk very slowly, leaning on his cane, about their yard, a modest expanse of tired, dry grass. His skin was taut and nut-brown, and, oddly, he reminded me of photos I'd seen of the mummies of Guanajuato, their skin stretched tightly from bone to bone. But his eyes were bright. They conveyed a quiet laughter that drew me over to the fence a number of times to chat with him. We communicated with few words, more English on his part than Spanish on mine, but the encounters were always warm.

The fence was one of your typical cheap California varieties, a steel mesh fence totally obliterated by a voracious evergreen ivy that snaked in and out the interstices and so completely knotted itself together that it was for all practical purposes totally ineradicable.

One day I showed the old gentleman some small round flat candies that I had bought in a Mexican grocery downtown. They were marvelously delicious to me, soft sweet brown caramel between what looked like communion wafers. The wrappers said something like Oblas de Dulce de Leche de Cabra. He explained that the candy was made from goat milk. Some weeks later the family disappeared for awhile, visiting relatives in Mexico. When they returned, the old man came to the fence with a paper bag for me, full of goat milk caramels made with communion wafers about five inches in diameter, more than twice as large as the ones I'd first encountered. I didn't see him in the yard very many times after that, and his son in law said he was not well.

The smaller disks were among the many Mexican candies that populated the interior of piñatas, I learned. My neighbors seemed to have many relatives or friends, with many children and many birthday parties. I enjoyed watching the backyard birthday parties at night, when I could shinny up my avocado tree and secretly watch the proceedings on the other side of the fence. The old grandfather would be seated, with one of his grandchildren leaning on his knee, his daughter beside him. The adult males would hang the piñata by a rope thrown over a high limb on their avocado tree, and the father or an uncle would be holding the working end. The little boy or girl, in suit or ruffles, would be blindfolded and given a stick to hit the piñata. But it would avoid all blows by being jerked quickly upward to a chorus of laughter and giggles, until the child, who hadn't learned that adults benevolently lie, was allowed to hit it broadside, spilling the sweets on the ground.

The car salesman, in shirt and tie, came running behind his wife, out of breath. "She's very upset," he said. "Her father is dying, and our telephone...doesn't work. But I think he's almost dead." His eyes sought mine above his wife's head.

What were the alternatives? 911, screaming ambulance, hospital hallways, doctors, priests, nurses, the tentacles of tubes in the nose, under the skin, catheters, bags of liquids, bags of blood, confusion, fright, insurance, bills....

"Why don't we have a look at him first, before we call," I said, and the husband pulled his wife with him up the sidewalk, as I followed. I had never been in their house before. A small grandchild was playing with his trucks in the hallway. The grandfather was lying in a ground level bunk bed, still alive but obviously very near death. His skin was yellowing. His daughter sat down on another small bed close by and continued weeping quietly. Her husband held the old man's head. I held his bare feet. A few minutes passed. And then between us there was a mere slight tremor and he was gone. In his own bed, with his family around him, and with a friend.

Later I saw the emergency unit pull up by the house. A medic got out, but walked, didn't run, to the house, and carried merely a clipboard.

Moriah's Visitor

MORIAH is a medium. She can see and talk to spirits. I would be more skeptical about this if it weren't for what happened the day that my friend Sandy and I had lunch with Moriah and her mom at Vinny Vanucci's in Galena.

We had met Moriah during the very short time she had a little teahouse just off Galena's main drag. She was young, buxom, pretty, with eyes bright and brown as a chipmunk's, and quick. She'd met her husband when she was digging a ditch during the Gulf War. Both were medics. He walked over to ask her a question, then stayed and stayed, and finally asked her out for dinner. Only later did she realize her shirt was unbuttoned.

Three astonishingly independent children later, she finally got the courage to speak openly about the spirits she had been able to see and hear since she was a child. She didn't want people to think she was nuts, so she had never talked about them. But at the time we met her she was "out," and she was doing spirit readings for weekend parties in Chicago.

The day I found faith in the everlasting afterlife was over spaghetti and meatballs at Vinny's in the second floor dining room. Moriah and her mother, Deb, and my partner, Sandy, and I were engaged in our usual chatter about the crazy things Moriah's kids had been doing, when Moriah suddenly looked over at me and said, "There's someone who wants to talk to you. He wants to apologize for something he said, and he's absolutely adamant."

I blinked and wasn't sure whether I should look behind me or not.

"Who is it?" I asked, thinking that might be a proper response. She wrinkled her smooth forehead and tried to translate whatever the gentleman was saying. She said he really wanted to apologize. This made no sense to me at all. I had the feeling that people were staring at a ghost standing behind me, and I sank down in my chair a bit, wishing he'd go away.

He was persistent, however, and tried another tack. Just words, nothing I could relate to. A meatball was staring at me.

And then Moriah said, "He says, 'mention the sleeveless beige belted jackets.'"

"Good God," I said. "It's Roger. Roger Levenson.

"Nobody knows about those jackets," I explained, "Not even Sandy. When Roger and I were together in Santa Barbara—he was my mentor in book arts, and I typeset his book on women printers for his publisher just before he died—one time we went to KMart together, and he found a belted safari-style, sleeveless jacket, a vest. He just loved it. So he bought one for him and one size smaller for me. After he died in San Francisco some years later, his executor friend mailed his jacket back to me. It's hanging in my attic closet in Galena, along with mine.

"But I can't think what he would want to apologize for," I mused. "I remember one time we were walking together down State Street in Santa Barbara, under the palms, and suddenly there was an explosion of swear words so heated and angry, I was afraid something terrible had happened to him. My adrenaline just shot skyward. And what was it all about? His shoe was untied."

But that was just Roger. Most of the time he was my loving friend and my exceedingly accurate walking encyclopedia for all aspects of book arts, opera, and trains, though I was never quite as interested in the trains as he was. He was the world authority on the Nevada County Narrow Gauge Railroad, if anybody cared. His book on women printers was the result of combing through decades of census reports and finding fine print on old invoices at ephemera shows. He demonstrated how very many women were employed in San Francisco in printing and typesetting work in the decades between the Civil War and turn of the century, and how their work linked with the women's movement. Tedious but interesting. He liked women printers and found me with two old printing presses in my garage late in his life.

Later that evening Moriah phoned. She was laughing. "He's so persistent, he won't let go. He showed up again while I was in the shower, insistent that I give you his apology."

Roger, the heavenly voyeur. He was a tough old bird with an eye for the ladies. I got a kick out of watching him wash his hair and put mousse on what was left of it, a few curling grey ends above his collar. He'd always wear a black beret over the balding part.

I can dig up from fading memory only a couple things he might have said that I didn't exactly like. One was true (I had gained a little weight), and the other was sad ("Why would you go sailing in bright sun with that loser when you would never sit on the beach with me under an umbrella?").

He gave me one of his black berets.

Its blue silk interior is faded, though the black felt is fine. There's an ornate coat of arms sewn inside that reads: "Beret de Luxe HOQUY, Foulard Impermeable, Pure Laine." I wear it a lot.

Hot Sauce

ARNIE was old and deaf, but that didn't stop him from wheeling and dealing in commercial Chicago real estate. He came with my first job in Chicago in 1963 with the Arbogust Company, a small advertising agency that specialized in writing and publishing newsletters for industrial firms. I started as a receptionist, sitting at the front desk with a view down a long, empty hallway.

One day a thin and listing figure sailed around a corner into view and tacked his way down the hall toward our glass door. The moment the tall thin old man came in he asked if anyone was free to telephone. Before I could answer, one of our women editors, who wore exquisitely tailored suits over an unfortunate hunchback, came quickly to the front. "I'm free, Arnie," she said. "Come back to my desk."

I could partially overhear a complex phone call involving whispers from Helen, quite audible statements from Arnie, and many pauses. Then he left, giving me a quick, polite wink as he took off on his winding way down the hall.

Helen explained, "He's quite deaf. But he still deals in real estate. He's a long time friend of Mr. Arbogust, and whenever he needs to make a phone call, we help him. If I'm not here, you can do it. All you have to do is repeat to Arnie what the person on the phone says. But you need to whisper and look directly at him. He's quite good at lip reading, and whispering seems to accentuate the lip movements. He's really a very nice man."

And he was. He hauled into our little harbor about once a week. For all I know, he might have had a secretary in a variety of ports for every day of the week.

In winter he wore a small, gray fedora perched rather high on his narrow, balding head. One day when he veered into our office and took off his hat, a white bandage crowned the apex, drawing, of course, all eyes.

We didn't know a lot about Arnie, except that he lived alone.

"It was a squirrel," he explained. "He got in my closet, and I was trying to get him out, and he jumped, and a shelf fell down on my head."

The three editors of the office were all trying to imagine, I'm sure, just how the squirrel had gotten into the house, but everyone was too polite to ask probing questions.

I was happy when I had the opportunity to make phone calls for Arnie, and we managed after a couple tries to be a fairly good team at the whispering and lip reading maneuvers.

The only male editor among the three was Bob O'Rourke, a tall, dark, and handsome young man who had recently married Lucy Bellagamba, who did have pretty legs and everything else, and he plunged heart first into a vivacious Mexican family. For the annual Christmas party my first year Mr. Arbogust asked Bob to choose a Mexican restaurant for the dinner. And Bob asked Lucy's father where we should go. And there we went.

I had never been to a Mexican restaurant before, having lived a sheltered small town life in rural Iowa amid fried chicken and roast beef.

The restaurant staff had laid a long, white cloth-covered table for us, set with plates, water and wine glasses, bowls of tortilla chips, and small bowls of fresh red sauces and fresh green sauces.

I was happily seated next to Arnie, and we immediately began to talk and whisper, and I whispered to him that I had never had Mexican food before and what should I try.

"Oh," he said, with a delighted smile, "This is the absolute best Mexican treat."

He reached for a tortilla chip, held it up before me, dipped it into the green sauce, which looked like macerated green grapes to me, showed me how he had piled up the green sauce on the chip, and popped it into his mouth. He chewed it, smiling happily, his eyes closed ecstatically.

"Ummmm!" he relished. "So good!"

Following his example, I loaded up a chip with green

sauce till it was spilling over the edges, chucked it entirely into my open mouth, clamped down on it, and just as the initiation by fire began, Arnie, grinning, reached for his water glass.

The Device

NORBERT SCHILLER liked to remind me, rather gleefully, that he had been born in the last century, in 1899, that he had occasionally glimpsed Emperor Franz Josef, and that he still remembered the scent of wild cyclamen in the Vienna Woods.

And I would ponder the fact that he was one of the actors in the first movie that scared the daylights out of me, when I was in high school in the 1950s, the original *The Thing*. He's a scientist in the film, doesn't say anything, just shows a handsome profile and a pipe. He landed parts like that because his exquisite knowledge of romantic German stage nuance did not transmute very well into everyday English in Hollywood.

His hands were as expressive as his voice, but aside from grand gestures, they were not very practical. He had no skills whatever with ordinary household tools. And he seemed distrustful of appliances. His idea of cleaning his shirts and trousers was to lay them over a backyard hedge in the sun. This worked for him, actually, quite well, because when he took the bus into downtown Santa Barbara or went to his room for a nap, his wife, younger than him and still a slim little sprite, would nab his clothes and throw them in the washing machine.

There was one device, however, that I owned which intrigued him immensely. It was my telephone answering machine. He discovered that if he called when I was out, he could provoke the little red light into blinking. He knew then that he would have, for a few moments at least, an attentive audience.

Consequently, I would return from grocery shopping or measuring a client's kitchen for a tile mural to find a message from Norbert.

At first, he would just say a few words on the tape such as, "Where ARE you, at this time of the day..." His extraordinary enunciation of this simple question would take my breath away. I can still hear his voice, the rise and fall of his faintly accented, deliciously nuanced phrasing. I would listen to his messages over and over, though I didn't tell him that.

He introduced me to Angelus Silesius through the tape recorder. He was a strange mystic from the 1600s who wrote slightly heretical rhyming couplets dealing with spiritual matters. Norbert would leave one of them on the recorder, and later we would attempt to translate it together, none too gracefully. One poor attempt read, "The rose your eye doth see today, hath bloomed within thy God alway."

I was happier when he planted poems on the machine.

His voice illuminated German lyric poetry. One of my favorites was a classic from Eichendorff that describes a beautiful moonlit night, "Und meine Seele spannte... And my soul reached out its wings, flying through the quiet countryside as though it were flying to its home."

Sometimes he would chant one of his own poems in his own odd English. This one was succinctly Norbert.

My home is my castle.
My boots are my car.
I sip sometimes coffee
And feel wunderbar.
A condo and a minium
Are both not for me.
I live on the minimum
And write poetry.

Once in a rare while there would be a song after the beep, a folk ballad from his youth or nostalgic songs about his beloved Vienna, or, in a husky voice very like Marlene Dietrich, he would sing, from the Blue Angel, "Ich bin von Kopf bis Fuss, auf Liebe eingestellt... I am from head to foot, made only for love."

I never told Norbert, but I didn't erase his phone messages. The machine used cassette tapes, and whenever he'd fill a tape, I'd put in a new one.

When you love someone in his mid-80s, you are very attuned to his mortal self. You know that the eyes, the voice, the unruly hair can dissipate at any moment into unglued molecules. Thus the devices humans have invented that capture a semblance, even just a shadow, of the beloved transient being are small and cherished miracles.

I still have those old tapes in a shoebox, with Norbert's lovely language interspersed with raucous beeps and squeaks.

Norbert's spiral notebook with the essence of his many lady loves.

The Bee Man

MY PARENTS' HOUSE was just across the street and down-hill from the old mechanics garage where my pottery shop was located in Audubon, Iowa. A block further downhill from my parents' house, Troublesome Creek, a poor, struggling vale of tears, wended its way through abandoned tires, chunks of cement, broken bottles, and a strange reddish sludge to reach one of the Nishna Botna tributaries.

Houses lining the scruffy edge of the creek bank were old, small, and in disrepair. One of them had window shades pulled down all around the house. Mr. Cole lived there alone. He was known as the bee man, because he was a beekeeper. He mostly kept to himself.

My pottery shop had a wooden garage door facing the street, through which cars used to be driven for mechanical work. It had a little door cut through the middle of it. When I first set up shop, a friend and I had painted a cheerful fairy tale forest scene on the big door. The little door appeared to be the entry into a large tree, with friendly rabbits peeking out from behind it.

In the summer time, I'd push the big door up out of the way and enjoy the warm breezes and the occasional folks who'd poke their heads in to see what I was working on. It was warm in the pottery, and I was usually barelegged and barefoot, powdered lightly with clay dust.

The beekeeper walked by almost every day, like clockwork, headed uptown. I'd always say "Hello" to him. He was quite tall, thin, and rangy. He was always clad in the light brown cotton shirts, trousers, and caps that my father, who also wore them, called "sun tans." They were no-nonsense workwear. "Bees don't like animal fibers," Mr. Cole explained to me one day. "I only wear cotton. It keeps them calm."

The bees apparently didn't notice his knee-high, tight-fitting, brown leather boots.

My father, recently retired from veterinary work, had great respect for Mr. Cole. He told me how one time when he was at a farm near the edge of town, the farmer pointed out a swarm of bees in the yard. Dad phoned Mr. Cole who drove out there immediately with a box of some sort. The bee man quietly reached into the swarm with his bare hands and picked up the bees.

He had another unusual talent. He played the violin. My mother, who was always digging for the creative vein in everyone, discovered it. Probably more to encourage him than to play herself, she got out her old violin from its ragged black cardboard case, and she'd practice a little and chat with him about fiddle playing. She was pretty awful, but she could manage an old Missouri hymn or two. She would trade ragged sheet music with Mr. Cole. It was never clear to either my mother or me how good a violin player Mr. Cole was, because he only played for himself, in his home. But it was a pleasant and neighborly connection between these two.

One evening I was sitting at my parents' kitchen table chatting with them over the remains of a light supper. There was a knock at the screen door, and my mother got up to answer it. Mr. Cole's voice entered the room. "I am sorry to put upon you at your supper time, but I wonder if you might have a G string you could loan me. I have broken mine and have no extras at the moment."

My father and I carefully studied the bread crumbs around the remaining slice or two of homemade white bread, while my mother got her violin case from under the bed. "Well, I thought I had one here," she muttered. "Oh, here it is." She took the scant little coil to the doorway, where Mr. Cole still stood outside on the stoop, having refused an invitation to enter. "Will this do?" she said.

"I am most grateful," he replied. "I will replace yours as soon as I can order a new one."

It was my mother, in her eternal creative quest, who found out that Mr. Cole knew some Spanish. She herself remembered enough Spanish from high school to sing *My Country Tis of Thee* in Spanish and recite most of *El Pobre*

Pollo, the story about the sky falling on the little chicken. That gave her one more topic of conversation with this intriguing neighbor, and she loaned him her sheet music for *La Paloma,* the dove.

We all had these tenuous connections with Mr. Cole, though much about him remained, and yet remains, mysterious. I had never had a chance to study Spanish, but I liked the idea. So I suggested to him one day that he bring me a Spanish phrase every day when he walked by, and I'd learn a little bit at a time. His gaunt and nearly toothless face wrinkled itself into a semblance of a smile.

He proceeded to bring me Spanish snippets for a week or so. There were two Spanish offerings he brought me which I remember to this day. One was a conjugation: "beso, besas, besa, besamos, besais, besan." I had to repeat that one several times for him before I got it right. He didn't tell me what it meant, only that it was a typical conjugation.

I'm not sure today that the grammar is quite right on his second sample, but this is exactly how I memorized it almost 40 years ago: "Su seguro servidor que besos sus manos y pies." "It's the polite way," he explained to me, "to sign a letter."

I looked up the words in my mother's Spanish dictionary one day, and it means, "your humble servant who kisses your hands and feet." The verb besar means to kiss.

Only years later did it ever occur to me that Mr. Cole's Spanish exemplars were very odd choices.

The Deer

$\mathcal{A}$ SALT-STREAKED CAR rounded the corner in Mineral Point with something I first thought were tree branches protruding from the trunk. I was headed for the Shake Rag Alley folk school with my camera, walking in the street as the night's freshening snow lay ankle-deep yet on all sidewalks. I glanced down at the rough and dirty ice I was attempting to traverse, then back to the passing car. The branches resolved themselves into four deer legs still connected, I assumed, to a dead animal, ignobly transported.

I went hunting only one time in my life, in 1967, somewhere near Wuppertal in, at that time, West Germany. I was attempting to be a teaching assistant in English at a girls school in Hagen-Haspe for a year. My ability to speak German was much worse than I had assumed going in, as my entire vocabulary was cribbed from the lyrics of Schubert and Wolf lieder, hardly the right words for a real world.

Among the farmers my veterinarian father served in rural Iowa was a family of German descent. When they heard from him that I was going to Germany, they told him I must visit their relative, Herr Mennenoh, who owned a lace factory near Wuppertal. And they made the connections.

I managed one weekend in autumn to get from Hagen to Wuppertal on the trains, and eventually to Herr Mennenoh's home in the countryside. It was not a large house, but I had learned by then that few Germans could ever hope to own any house at all. Frau Mennenoh, a gray-haired motherly sort, was very kind to me and gave me a green carrying bag trimmed with colorfully woven bands, apparently what had been meant by "lace making."

We had a quiet supper of bread and cheese in a small room, the walls of which were decorated with a great many deer horn plaques. I don't remember any heads, just horns. Frau Mennenoh showed me a few pieces of jewelry in a drawer, each brooch encompassing an ivory deer tooth in its design.

Herr Mennenoh was a very gentle man. He must have been in his middle or late seventies, grey haired, very slim, still standing straight, though with just the faintest forward bow. He spoke a careful English with me, tilting his head with a faint smile.

It was soon apparent to me that the deer on the wall and in the woods were his main love. He suggested that we go hunting together the next day. I wasn't too happy at the thought of seeing a deer killed, but I was up for it at dawn.

Herr Mennenoh now was dressed in a loden green wool

outfit, a jacket with a little factory trim, and pants buckled just below his knees, with high wool stockings and sturdy shoes. His grey-green wool hat had a little brush on it. He carried a rifle.

I'm not at ease in the presence of guns, as my father never had one in the house, but Herr Mennenoh smiled and nodded at me, and we walked off together into the forest that covered high hills behind the house.

We walked silently on a little trail through the woods, stepping carefully around sticks and leaf piles and pausing now and then to look and listen as the sun spangled through the beech trees. There were no deer in sight. I breathed a little easier.

We walked on into deep pine forest but Herr Mennenoh now seemed more interested in talking about deer than shooting them. He told me that he did not own the land we were walking through, but he had the sole rights for hunting on the property. With his right to hunt deer came quite a few responsibilities. He was expected to keep watch on the deer herd and to know how many bucks, does, and fawns there were. He would be allowed to shoot a certain number each year in order to keep the herd from overpopulating his designated forest area.

In addition, in winter he was expected to bring hay to feed the deer. There was a part of the forest that had been logged and then replanted with little pines. If the deer were so hungry they nibbled on the baby trees, he would have to pay for the financial loss. Thus he made sure there was plenty of winter food for the herd.

We returned to the house without ever seeing a deer.

We sat down at the table with coffee and cakes. "The deer, die Rehe," Herr Mennenoh said, "are a very special animal. They are revered. You know the word for people eating?"

"Yes," I answered. "Essen. Wir essen. We eat."

"And what about the word for animals?"

"I know that, too," I said. "It's fressen. Die Hunde fressen. The dogs eat."

There's something ugly about this word. If you want to portray a disgusting, uncouth human being in German, that's one of the words you can use to describe his eating habits. It makes a man sound animalistic.

"But the deer have their very own verb," continued Herr Mennenoh. "They don't eat like other animals. They graze delicately. Die Rehe äsen." When he spoke those words, die Rehe äsen, he said them so slowly and lovingly that I could see the gentle creature of his mind lower its head, nudge the grass aside with one small, curving hoof, then neatly select a white wildflower with its little teeth and soft lips.

Continuing my walk toward Shake Rag Alley, I passed Karl's corner liquor store, covered in metal signs offering bargains on Budweiser beer. Another sign indicated that this was a CDW station for checking the brains of hunted deer for mad deer disease. On less snowy weekends during Wisconsin's deer season often there's a row of pickups, each with a dead deer slung in the back, waiting in line at the back of the liquor store to do the state's paperwork.

Shake Rag Alley shimmered, a winter painting in snow, the log cabin, the old cottages, the winding paths of the local folk school were all sheathed in luminous white. It was early yet, and white hoar frost softly encrusted every twig and bough, lightly sparkling in the morning sun.

Stepping carefully along a hidden path, I saw the rustic cedar railing that leads up hill toward the summer stage. My boots marked each step's location in the snow. The stage, three or four feet above the ground, extends out from a high limestone quarry wall.

At the edge of the seating area, other footprints preceded mine. Smaller. Two sets of hooves had walked here, one larger, with the hoof splits pointing straight forward, a buck, and the other, that of a doe, smaller, with more curve and less space in the bifurcation. They had lain in the snow, in a packed down nest. And one had pissed in the snow.

I followed the tracks. The doe had jumped onto the snow blanketed stage and walked directly to the center to face an eastern audience. She then leaped from the stage over the center steps onto the runway, down the center aisle, through the rear wall of arbor vitae—and away.

Your Eyes

It's a long story how I got there, but I was with a Spanish teacher from my small town Iowa high school, his wife, her young boy, and an exchange student from Switzerland, and we were among the happy sardines packed into a big motel banquet hall in Saltillo, Mexico.

It was New Year's Eve. Everything was festive and full of color. Bright ribbons and lacey, pastel papercuts swung from the ceiling. Confetti curls in multi-hued tangles wove in and out of the plates set before us on the long tables.

We ate sweet things I had no name for. I spoke no Spanish but I relished the small, sugared breads and cookies.

I had my eye on a man and a woman sitting at a very small table near the mariachi band, sipping their drinks. Both were silver-haired, of indeterminate age. The woman was tall and thin, with pale skin. She wore a red dress jacket, fitting tight at the waist, with a long red skirt, slit halfway up the thigh. The man wore a black suit and tie and had an aristocratic look. At one point, the woman leaned across the little table, slapped him on both cheeks, and then kissed him.

When the band started to play dance tunes, they were the first couple on the floor.

Eventually, midnight arrived, with a musical countdown and a wallop on drums and fanfare on trumpets. Everyone cheered. Everyone stood up and milled around, hugging and kissing all the people within arms' reach. This general embrace went on for a good while, but finally the band started up again with more dance music, and the crowd shifted into dancing pairs.

I didn't go back to the table, partly because someone had taken my seat. I was lagging as well, hoping I might get to dance. An elderly Mexican man gave me a slight bow and held out his dusky hand. We danced. He was a few inches shorter than me. He spoke no English, I spoke no Spanish.

It was fun, and we smiled happily at each other. The dance floor was so crowded we could barely turn around. But we kept on gliding and turning, smiling and laughing.

"Sus ojos," he said, softly, with a shy look into my blue eyes, as we spun warmly around in the melting melee.

When the song was over, relatives were reaching for him, and I had spotted my companions as well.

Later, back in the states, I checked a Spanish-English dictionary, and I'd guessed right.

The Gun

THE SALES REPS from South Dakota never took their cowboy hats off when all the TCI dealers went out to Johnnie's Club for dinner. They ate their steaks with their hats on, and the few ladies there in the early evening who paid attention maybe got a hat dance by the juke box later.

Tully, who owned Talbot Carlson, Inc., always gave the visiting salesmen a fine time. He could have chewed them out and pounded them, and they still would have looked upon that man with reverence.

He was tall, and he seemed taller than he actually was. It was some kind of perceptive illusion. The man had charisma, that was what it was. He had curly, graying Irish hair, a ruddy complexion in a square strong face, and a bull neck over broad shoulders. He wore well-fitted western shirts with delicate tiny flower prints and pearl buttons, prominent belt buckle, and western pants that broke at the perfect place against his expensive cowboy boots.

One of the distributors for the TCI cattle minerals said

once, "It's worth it to bring the guys all the way down here just to watch That Man walk across the room."

When Tully got up in front of the dealers to talk, all was silence. He'd step to the podium and grasp its sides in his hands. He'd lean that bull neck slightly forward, and, without changing his grip or moving his head, he'd talk, without notes, and quite articulately. His rapt audience would feel energized, "rarin' to go," when he finished.

One night at Johnnie's Club I was sitting at a small table with Jud and Bill, the two marketing managers on staff, who both traveled a lot. Jud carried a different style of cowboy hat for every state he serviced. Bill tested new recruits by introducing them to an old farm dog he trusted. Tully was sitting at the bar with his back to us. There was a mirror behind the bar, and I was sitting where I could watch his face. I wanted to dance with him. About the time I'd given up on that, he stood up, not looking at me, went over to the juke box, and methodically plunked in a succession of quarters. Then he strode over to our table and held out his hand, "Would you dance with me?"

He was a good dancer, I was happy to find, and we danced several fast and slow ones, and then he swooped me up in his arms, deposited me back at my table, and announced, "The Lake House is now open for those of you still on your feet." And he left.

So we all exited Johnnie's Club and repaired to the Lake House, which was a garage on the alley behind Tully and

Kay's house which he had turned into a lounge bar, exceedingly well-stocked with good whisky. I should have gone home at that point but I didn't, mesmerized by Tully like the rest.

I don't like whisky so I was in no danger of drunkenness, but the rest of the party were not so afflicted. Gradually the lower level salesmen stumbled off to their motel rooms, leaving the core of distributors and local marketing staff. Tully's secretary had gone home. I was the only woman left. There was plenty of good-natured, increasingly drunken teasing.

"Did you show her your gun, Tully?" one of them called out. The others joined in, "Yeah, Tully, show her your gun!" I was wondering just what they all had in mind.

Tully grabbed my hand and dragged me out of the Lake House and in large steps to the back door of the house. Inside, in a hallway, were rows of drawers against the wall. He jerked one open and took out a large black pistol wrapped in soft cloth. "This is a 45 magnum," he said, and dropped it into my hands. I nearly fell to the floor holding on to it, it was so heavy. I handed it right back to him.

"You think you know me," he said, "but you don't know what power I have with this gun." He staggered a little and waved the gun over his head. "With this gun I can kill anything. I can shoot the president. I can kill a dog. I can..."

While I was watching him, fascinated and a little frightened, Tully's wife, Kay, came from the house interior into the hallway. With a calm, steady voice, she said, "Now, Tully, we won't have any of that. Put the gun away. And take Judy back to the party."

A little embarrassed, I trudged after him back to the Lake House. Several more distributors had slipped away during our absence, and now only his two sales managers and I were left. He gathered us near him and launched into energetic questioning of the two men about sales potentials of the various Midwest states. I was sitting next to him on the couch, and any time I started to speak, he'd lightly touch my hands and say, "Just shush."

This went on endlessly, as the eyelids of Jud and Bill grew red and drooping. At long last, the sun came up, and he released the two poor guys, who'd been grilled unmercifully for hours. They left. "Well," he said.

I got up to leave, too. I stood in the screen door looking back at him and wondering. He looked as fresh and fine as he'd looked on the dance floor earlier. He put his arms behind his head, leaned his long body back against the couch, and said, "You know that since we first met I have wanted to spend a night with you. This is as close as I could come."

I pushed the screen door open, then stepped back inside. "It's very hard to close a door once it's been opened," I said.

"It's not closed," he said. "But I cannot do what I want."

The Cane

Jowa City, in the fall and in the rain. Walking from Old Capitol toward Currier Hall, I was absorbed by the yellow leaves in the puddles, how dark the rain water was in the deeper pools, the blackness of the elms.

In my first months at the university, I had found a friend at the dorm. Nopbha's eyes were dark and soft. She had short, black, curling hair and wore long skirts, sometimes a sarong. She took small steps and swayed lightly as she walked with me down the dormitory hall to dinner. English was not easy for her, but she punctuated all that she said with her small brown hands, flitting lightly like butterflies about my hands, my arms, my face. Sometimes she would hold my hand as we walked together, leaning lightly against me. The other girls might look at us a bit askance, as we crowded near the dining hall doors, waiting for them to open, but I was too engrossed in the mysterious Orient to care.

She was a graduate student in mathematics, from Bangkok. She explained to me one time, "Our teacher tell us that if we are lucky to go to America, study mathematics, she tell boys in class not to hold hands in America. Americans not understand."

Her teacher had apparently restricted the warning only to boys.

One afternoon Nopbha said she needed to buy aspirin, so I accompanied her on the stroll downtown, scuffing through the leaves. A little girl, about kindergarten age, in a yellow coat, was playing in the lawn near a large house. As we walked by, arm in arm, the child looked up and said, "What do you have your arm around that girl for?"

Nopbha turned and answered her, "Because we love each other." As we walked on, I wondered to myself how and why a small child could so early absorb a culture's subtle taboos.

Nopbha was dating a young Thai student. I asked what she looked for in a man. She said, saying the syllables softly, distinctly, "De-li-cate fee-ling."

My friend went home with me at Christmas to my small western Iowa town, and we went sledding with my parents and my sister. We were all very merry cascading down the hills on our saucer sleds. Nopbha, of course, had never played snow games in Thailand, and my sister and I decked her out with the old wool snow suits we'd outgrown. She was so small and slim.

I played my new LP for her, "The King and I," and I spun and bumped around our small living room with my favorite song, "Shall We Dance." Nopbha carefully examined the record album and its photographs. She was curious about it because it was forbidden in Thailand, she said, though she didn't explain why.

My mother cooked overwhelmingly generous dinners of ham and turkey, gravies, sage dressing, canned fruit and vegetables from their summer garden, and all the cranberry trimmings and pumpkin pie. Only much later did I find out that Nopbha was vegetarian. "It all right," she explained. "In Buddhism we try not to hurt. Should not make your mother unhappy. So I don't say."

I thought of many things to not say after Nopbha returned with her masters degree to Thailand. Many things not to be so certain about.

There was a Ben Franklin store in downtown Iowa City, and occasionally I had an egg salad sandwich there. I liked to sit at the U-shaped counter, alone, and watch the venerable waitresses whisking briskly back and forth with heavy white mugs and plates.

One afternoon I was sipping leisurely through a lemonade, contemplating across from me a bleached old man. Nopbha had asked me once why in America old people didn't live with their families, as was the norm in Thailand. I didn't know an answer. My own grandparents in Kansas and Missouri were long gone, and old folks in my home town mostly ended up in the nursing home, a prelude to the cemetery. I knew hardly any old people then, and I wondered what it was like to be old. Anywhere.

The old man across from me was alone. He didn't seem to notice anything around him. He merely gazed at the counter, his cup, his spoon, unmoving. I wondered if he had a family and where he lived. Did anyone care for him?

Suddenly from below the counter a small brown hand reached up and tapped him on the chest. I was startled. The fingers of the hand were pointed and delicate. They held a child's ball. Turning on his stool as slowly as a music box figure runs down, the old man faced finally sideways. He placed his large, pale hand over the small, brown one, and, leaning his weight upon it, he hobbled away.

Nopbha Buranakul at my parents' cabin in the woods 1960.

White Pigeons

I DROVE through Brayton in the early dusk. First little Iowa town north of I-80 on the old, two-lane Highway 71. Ruins of the old town hall cling right to the edge of the road.

All that's left is a ragged white stucco foundation. Holes where the windows used to be. When it was still alive and lively, you had to mount a big staircase to the first floor doors. Inside was a large, open room with wood flooring. It was the community dance hall for every wedding and anniversary for miles around, the best dancing and gathering place in this heavily Danish county of farmers.

Heavily Danish maybe isn't quite the right phrase, but maybe it is, too. The Danes always eat well. The dance floor and the whole shebang collapsed during a dance one night roughly thirty years ago. Nobody got killed, and over the next year or so all the wood and plaster were gradually hauled away, leaving just the foundation, by itself, empty.

I only went to one dance there, and I'm not exactly sure how I got up the courage to go all alone. Must have been curiosity. And I do like dancing, even if it's mostly polkas in that neck of the woods.

After college, after four years working in Chicago and an incoherent year in Germany, I came back to my hometown, Audubon, ten miles north of Brayton, and went into business as a potter, even though, initially, I couldn't make a teapot more than an inch high. But I'd read Ayn Rand's *Atlas Shrugged* and figured I could do anything.

When I got tired of living with my parents, I discovered an old Carpenter Gothic house on the wrong side of the tracks—there were still actually tracks then, though they dead-ended at Roberts Feed & Seed. The house was up for county auction by way of unpaid taxes of about $900. I didn't have $900 but I had a little jewelry box full of rings I'd bought with my first paychecks in Chicago. I went to Dad and asked if he'd loan me $900 and handed him the rings for collateral. He went for it. "Sounds like bargain real estate to me," he said. I was the only one at the auction and got the old gray house, paint all worn off, for my own.

It was definitely a good real estate bargain. Especially since Dad gave me the rings back. "I don't have a whole lot of use for these," he said, and he added, "I'll help you paint it if you want. I think if I hook up our old vacuum sweeper backwards, we could spray it pretty fast."

It was a two-story house with the remains of sunburst doodads in the gables, six cedar trees, two bramble bushes (one with asparagus sharing its rootroom), and a carriage house painted barn red, under an old box elder tree.

The carriage house must have been fairly elegant in its day. There was a little room inside one corner with the cobwebbed remains of a two-holer. There was a fairly large area for a workshop. And there was a shed-roofed garage for a buggy on one end, just right for my little red VW bug. Built into the gable overlooking the garage roof was a dovecote. Somebody must have kept pigeons. There were little entry portals for the birds under a window that looked out into the box elder. I had to go inside the barn and climb up a ladder nailed to a wall to get up in the dove cote. I washed it all out and put in a sleeping bag. I liked to sneak up there in the dark on really hot summer nights to sleep. I'd wake up surrounded by the conversations of sparrows in the box elder as we all watched the sun rise over the hulking grain bins of the co-op on the east side of the creek.

Maybe it was an anniversary dance for someone I knew or my veterinarian father knew. At least the Brayton town hall was somewhere interesting to go on a wintry night. I sat around on a folding chair for a long time just watching, since most people there were married couples and danced together.

One older farmer in faded blue bib overalls and thin, slicked-back grey hair, must have recognized me, and he asked me to dance. He was a little bow-legged, but we did a couple good polkas together until we were both out of breath.

We sat down together on the side.

I asked him about his farm. "Well, I raise purebred Angus," he said. "Pretty good herd. Your dad saved a couple calves for me. He was always good natured at having to come out in the middle of the night."

But what he really loved were his pigeons, he confided. "I raise white pigeons, don't you know. I have quite a few. Those white pigeons wheeling over the farm yard are sure a sight," he said, with a broad smile.

And then he continued, "Your dad's reserved one white pair for you, come spring," he said.

And then, he halted and looked quizzically at me—"I haven't told a secret, have I?"

And he had.

My veterinarian father, around 1972.

Irish Spring

THE IDEA of printing a book intrigued me at least as much as writing one. I read the ad in the *Santa Barbara News Press* a couple times. It offered an antique 8x10 Chandler & Price printing press. I measured the corners of my garage tile painting studio and thought that something eight by ten feet was going to take up about half the space, but I went to look at the press anyway.

It was a small black iron thing, a little bigger than a breadbox, with a flat, round ink spreader and a lever like a one-armed bandit. The ink rollers ran across a small iron frame eight inches by ten inches into which one could set type or woodcuts. I bought it.

Somehow I figured out how to make it work. And I amused myself for many a night making small linocuts for a little book based on a humorous poem about a drunken sea captain whose survey of early Santa Barbara resulted in mismatched streets.

A catalog of typefaces from a Los Angeles foundry had been bundled with the press and its gadgetry. I ordered a font of metal type in Goudy Oldstyle, which looked pretty good to me. I set a paragraph of introductory material and was astonished to find that three quarters of the way through I ran out of "e's." That was about four years before the Macintosh and Apple Laserwriter revolutionized typesetting for the printing industry and for ordinary folks, as well. Today's typesetters and emailers have an infinite supply of e's.

I bought a second font of Goudy Oldstyle type, printed the little book, and bound a few copies. After that the 8x10 size began to feel constraining. I discovered that a larger press, a Vandercook proof press, was still in the shop of a printer in a northwest Iowa town for whom I'd sold color brochures prior to moving to Santa Barbara. The owner said he'd happily sell me that press, and he crated and shipped it to my garage in Santa Barbara.

This press, about six feet long and weighing half a ton, had a flat bed on which the type or woodcuts were placed and a drum and roller assembly that rolled over them. It would print an area 13 inches by 20 inches. I had difficulty getting the thing to work right. It wouldn't grab the paper predictably, and I didn't know how to control the impression. Some places would be light and some dark. Nothing I tried corrected matters. And the press sat there stolidly, daring me to tame it.

I knew no printers, no one who would understand this

recalcitrant beast. So I started going to Friends of the UCSB Library lectures, hoping that in that rarified academic atmosphere, among people who treasured well-made books, I might find some help.

I lucked out.

The first lecturer I heard was Roger Levenson, who had been the proprietor of Tamalpais Press in Berkeley and taught book arts at the university's Bancroft Library. He had recently retired to Santa Barbara. After his lecture on the Grabhorn brothers, fine, limited edition printers in San Francisco, I attempted to talk to him. He had cornered the Special Collections director and was gesturing broadly, his voice stentorian. He wore a red silk vest. A black beret was clamped down over thin, longish gray hair. He was about my height and stocky, with an aquiline nose, drooping cheeks, stern eyes, and an imposing voice that overrode all others. Many of his sentences began with a thrusting "You have to understand—" He was a born lecturer, on or off the podium.

He ignored my presence until he heard me say in a small voice that I had a Vandercook. And then he turned suddenly to me, all ears and eyes, totally attentive. The Special Collections director took the occasion to flee. Roger Levenson asked, in a gruff voice, "What in the world are you doing with a printing press?"

I explained that I, actually, had two of them and had printed a small book on the Chandler & Price but was unable to figure out how the Vandercook worked. "What kind of type have you got?" he asked me.

"I have two fonts of Goudy Oldstyle," I said, "but it doesn't go very far."

"That's old hat. You should be using something with more style," he said, "something more unusual, like the typeface Frederic Goudy designed for the University of California. I bet I could get hold of some of it for you."

He walked out of the lecture hall with me. "What are you trying to print with that Vandercook?"

"I've been making linocuts for a short story by Norbert Schiller that I want to make into a book. I haven't actually set any type yet."

"Don't use that Goudy Oldstyle," he commanded. "I'll call Mackenzie & Harris in San Francisco tomorrow and see if they can stir up any University of California Oldstyle for you. You need a typeface with pizzazz." I wasn't getting a word in edgewise, so I just kept nodding assent.

"Where do you live?" he went thundering on. "When can I see your press? I could come by your house tomorrow afternoon after I've snoozlecated on the beach awhile. I'll bring my tools, and we'll have a look at it."

I felt like I'd rubbed Aladdin's lamp and gotten way more than I'd wished for.

He came to check on that press almost every day.

What first appeared a simple registration correction somehow became more complex, and Roger had to order little gizmos, and we had to get together frequently to try different ways of setting up the packing.

He was a born teacher. There was nothing he loved more than to teach printing and all aspects of book arts, printing presses, history of printing, history of type design, how Gutenberg's type molds worked. Everything. And I was the eager student, so happy to have found exactly the teacher I'd wished for.

One day, several weeks after I'd met him, we were both bent over the press, he trying to delicately adjust something, swearing cheerfully, and me trying to hold the roller assembly steady. We were very close together. He smelled very clean, like Irish Spring soap. I bit him on the back of the neck. He didn't say anything.

Later we went in the house and sat together on the couch and talked about it. "I'm 69," he said. "You know, I came to Santa Barbara to languish in the elephant graveyard and sit on the beach. I didn't expect to find you."

He thought about it a little more. "If I'd known I was going to meet you, I wouldn't have given away all my colored inks."

Roger Levenson was exceptionally knowledgeable about book arts, opera, and trains. He loved the old steam locomotives.

myself a little ahead of the leader and an unknown dear old lady at my side who kept silent but even pace with my long strides. A sudden gust of wind made her open her arms wide, exclaiming with an almost infectious conviction, "Oh, I am so tired of it all! How I wish I could fly!"

A page from the book I illustrated and printed, a short story by Norbert Schiller.

Stealing Persimmons

THE PHONE RANG late one golden afternoon in Santa Barbara. It was Norbert Schiller. "I know you're working," he said, his German accent leaning into persuasive mode, "But it's such a beautiful day. Let's go steal persimmons. I know the tree."

I put away my glazes and brushes. I backed my little red VW bug out onto Cliff Drive and drove over to the house where Norbert, in his mid 80s, lived with Mary, his much younger wife. Mary was always happy to have me entertain Norbert.

And off we went, at Norbert's direction, to the Natural History Museum, located in a beautiful grove of old valley oaks. Mottled sunlight fell softly on the stucco buildings and on their orange-hued tile roofs. Norbert's criminal instincts were good. There were no other cars in the parking lot.

We parked way down at the far end, where a little gate led into a scruffy and neglected area of trees and weeds.

Norbert extricated himself slowly from the front seat.

He had brought with him a couple good-sized gunny sacks. He wasn't wearing his usual leather visor, since the sun was rapidly descending. He ruffled his grey hair with his hand, standing it up on end.

There was a haphazard trail beyond the gate, not much used, but we followed it. Norbert in his cords and Birkenstocks walked slowly, while I danced around in front of him. He was watching the ground rather carefully, making sure where he put his feet.

Suddenly he looked up. "There it is," he said.

The last longing rays of the sun penetrated the grove and lit the tree, laden with large, bright orange persimmons. They glowed like the golden apples Freya grew for the gods of Valhalla, source of their eternal lives.

We picked the fruit hanging within reach. These were the kind of persimmons that are rather erotic looking, shaped very much like a woman's breast, as Norbert deigned to mention more than once and most appreciatively. On the stem end, they have four green sepals, connected and very symmetrical, a little like a pointy four leaf clover. And just as lucky for the finders.

I thought we probably had enough. Norbert, in everything else, was more than satisfied with just the "essence," but in this case, he wanted it all. So I climbed up into the tree's branches, among the darkening green shadows, and continued to hand down to Norbert the beautiful fruit. He gently placed each one in his burlap bags. When those were full, he put a few last fruit inside his shirt. I made two trips hauling the heavy sacks to the car.

On the way home Norbert told me that there's a cliche phrase in German about friendship that goes something like, "He's the kind of friend you can steal peaches with."

I can't say that I'm overly fond of persimmons as human food, though okay for Norbert and the gods. You have to wait until they soften, and then they suddenly get real gooey, like bright orange jam.

I took three of them home with me. Norbert and Mary ate the rest of the harvest.

Frances Holden in the 1930s.

Scotch and Synchronicity

I WAS HELPING Frances Holden with the booksale on the seventh floor of the UCSB library in Santa Barbara. Frances, who was in her late 80s, had run the sales of donated books for many years. Consequently, she had first choice of purchase. She was also a major donor to the library and could do as she pleased. She had ten rooms of floor-to-ceiling books in the old rambling house she owned on several acres above the ocean in Hope Ranch. I had second choice. I amused myself looking for German books with attractive type and illustrations.

"Handle this, will you?" Frances said to me. She had her eye on a couple students and the possibility of selling them some slightly outdated travel books. She was a small-boned woman with an indeterminate, thickened waist and short, straight, unmanageable hair, rarely seen in any mirror. She had a gruff looking, squarish face and a brusque voice to match.

A dark-haired young woman handed me her selection

and the money for it. It was a handsome book in German that I had looked at carefully, earlier. I complimented her on her choice and asked about her interest in things Germanic.

"I have a friend who is German," she said. "He's old but quite a gentleman. He used to work in the theater in Germany but left when Hitler came in. He worked with the director Pabst and the actress Louise Brooks."

"That's interesting," I replied. "I had a German friend from that era, also. But he died recently."

"Would you like to meet him?" the woman asked. "He enjoys company. His name is Rudolf Joseph, and he's in the Montecito phone book. Just call him up and introduce yourself."

"Thanks," I said. "Maybe I will."

But I knew I would most definitely not.

I was not about to befriend another elderly German. I'd just lost one. Norbert Schiller, born in Vienna in 1899, actor in German theaters in the twenties and early thirties, and my friend. He had just died, age 88, after lying in bed and disintegrating for months and months. No fun there.

And Frances was no spring chicken, either, though she drove like one. Her old ivory Buick had one big slick leather seat across the front and no seat belts. I never felt safe in that car. "Stop worrying," she'd growl. "No one would dare hit this car. It's built like a tank."

After we counted up the book sale take, we headed for her house in her car. As she barrelled that Buick down the entrance ramp onto the freeway, her tiny feet in sensible shoes barely reaching the pedals, she ripped off her glasses and handed them to me. "I can't see anything out of these," she complained. "Can you clean them off?"

I was relieved when we turned into her driveway and pulled into the old garage draped in bougainvillea. My little Volkswagen was parked nearby. We sat outside in her porch swing for a while, shaded by clusters of trees and rampant vines in a soft late afternoon glow. Frances looked at me. "How about a hotdog and some scotch?" she inquired.

I lied and said I wasn't hungry. "Maude!" she yelled towards the kitchen, and her housekeeper appeared, nodded, returned with scotch for Frances, red wine for me.

A terra cotta bust of Lotte Lehmann on a pedestal caught the dappling shadows of early evening. Lotte was the German opera singer Frances had lived with for decades in this house, among these extensive gardens, until her death some years ago.

Later, as I chugged my red VW bug into the asphalt driveway of my own little flat-roofed house on Cliff Drive, I spotted something behind the ferns shading the front door. It was a long cardboard tube left by the postman. It had German stamps and a return address I didn't recognize.

I took it inside and carefully extracted a gigantic movie poster in yellow and black. It advertised the silent film Pandora's Box, directed by Pabst. Most of the poster was taken up by the profile of Louise Brooks. Her short, sleek black hair fit her head like a helmet, with bangs curving all the way to her eyebrows. She had one of the great looks of the twenties.

There was a note with the poster, written in a shaky hand. It was from one of Norbert's long-ago fans, who had located him a few months ago after all these many years since he was a heartthrob on the stage in Frankfurt, Berlin, and Munich. The woman had sent Norbert one last evocative letter of adoration. He had smiled weakly from his bed and asked me to write something nice to her.

She had sent me the poster as a thank you for my letter.

I shook my head in disbelief. Norbert. Louise Brooks. Pabst. All in one day? I shivered.

I reached for the Montecito phone book.

Little Horses

BEFORE he lost it all, he had it all. All the pretty little horses. They were slightly larger than Shetlands, but, unlike Shetlands, perfectly proportioned. One of the herds ran in the waving grasses of a prairie he had started, planting rich corn land with Indian grass, big blue stem, and every wild seed he could find along the old railroad tracks.

Wink's ponies were all very tame. He talked to them and touched them. He brought a couple ponies, dappled in black and white patches, near the old house with the green roof for me to see. While examining the foot of one, he bumped into the other, muttering, "Excuse me!"

Before his father died and left him alone in the house with the green tile roof his grandfather had built, they used to race chariots around the Iowa State Fair track in front of the grandstand. "We each had a span of four horses, black or white, and we had sheets pinned on for togas," he recalled, showing me photographs. The chariots resided in an out-building on the farm, along with a circus calliope, stage-

79

coach, buckboards, and several brightly painted carriages, all sized perfectly for the little horses to pull.

He was a good dancer, but maybe not the best legislator at the state capitol in Des Moines. I was more interested in his ability to waltz than in his rantings about capital punishment. We'd met dancing. He was a handsome man in his dark hair and his western style suit, a few years older than me. Our bodies danced well together, and after the dance, we continued in a haystack under a harvest moon.

The next morning, to my amusement, he realized he'd lost his belt. He was in a hurry to get back out to the haystack before his hired man showed up to pitch hay.

He invited me to one of his annual pony sales. I sat on the bleachers amid a small crowd of people bidding on his yearly excess. The best one, the one he hoped would bring in some big dollars, was a little gray stallion with a silky, white tail drifting almost to the dirt floor of the arena. Bidding was slow, and suddenly Wink, wearing a handsome western jacket and hat, leaped onto the bare back of the pony and, standing, rode him galloping around the ring. But it didn't work. The stallion was sold for only $200.

I moved away from Iowa some time after that. He wasn't much for writing. Things began to fall apart in rural Iowa in the 1980s. He lost the election. He lost the farm. He lost his grandfather's house. He took up religion. A friend told me he had married his housekeeper.

One day I saw a photo in the *Santa Barbara News Press*

Wink and one of his multitude of ponies, in a linocut
I carved in the mid–1970s.

illustrating the despair of Midwest farm communities. There was Wink with his pregnant wife beside a teepee, where they were living and where they intended to live with the oncoming baby.

I tried once to write to him and received a polite thank you signed by his wife. I heard through the grapevine that there were now three children and they were living in a house but had no money. They had a few ponies and gave rides to children who were physically or mentally challenged.

Not long ago I went to the Iowa State Fair for the first time in nearly 30 years. I was curious about something on the fair map titled Grandfather's Barn. It was at the top of the hill, a small barn with a group of small caged animals and chickens that would never be cooped up together on a real farm. A large door opened to a backyard.

An old man, thin and stooped, with a foot long white beard, was leading a desultory pony around and around in a circle. I don't think he could see very well.

A photo I took of Wink and a kitten. He loved animals, and they responded in kind.

The Audubon Fire Dept.

GIRLS WORE SKIRTS when I was in grade school in Audubon, Iowa, in the early 1950s. Except for the deep snow days requiring snow pants, I walked across town to school in skirts every day in winter, even though my knees were frosty. We thought nothing of it. It was the way things were.

I liked to walk up the back alley from our house to Main Street, then squeeze through an eighteen-inch secret passageway littered with interesting junk between two old brick buildings. I emerged in downtown central next to the never-to-be-entered Iowa Liquor Store, where only drunks and bad people went inside. They carried out surreptitious brown sacks, and my mother had warned me to stay away from people like that.

Main Street was an uphill walk, but there was always a good chance of seeing Jimmie Blake in the next block. He might be coming out of the Hamburger Shop or the newspaper office about the time we kids were hoofing it to school.

Jimmie earned pin money by taking Rose Theatre schedules and funeral cards around to the stores along the three blocks of mercantile business. I don't know how old he was. He was an adult, but he was like another child to us, one who could do tricks. I saw him pull quarters out of many a kid's ear. He always wore overalls and a blue cotton shirt. He'd show us the shiny fireman's badge pinned on his overalls, and we were suitably impressed, every time. Sometimes, if we weren't in a hurry, he'd show us the little spiral notebook he had in one of his overall pockets. It contained a running list of all the fires in town in pencil. The chief or one of the firemen would always update it for him. He liked fires and firetrucks.

Jimmie was always happy.

And he was happiest of all at the movies. The man who owned the Rose Theatre let him go to all the movies for free. When my parents took my sister and me to a movie, we'd munch popcorn and watch Jimmie until the show started. He always sat way down in front, and he'd be looking every few moments at his big wristwatch. He could tell time. At least he knew where the hands should be at 7:00 when the movie should start. The high school kid in the projection room was not always as precise about starting times. Jimmie would be down there in front, half turned around so he could see the little lighted window of the projection box. He'd look at his watch, and the moment the big hand was straight up, he'd chop his right arm down, like someone starting a foot race. Nothing would happen, and he'd have to give the signal several times before the kid upstairs would "get it" and roll the film.

Grade school, high school, college, four years in Chicago, a year in Germany. And then I returned to my home town to start up a pottery business. Hardly anything had changed in all those years. The Iowa Liquor Store was gone, and the Ben Franklin store with the mynah bird and goldfish. But Jimmie was still there, his dark hair now streaked with gray. Still wearing the old overalls and the badge. His parents had died, and now he lived at the Friendship Home, but he was on Main Street, still, almost every day.

The first summer I was back, I was startled one sunny afternoon to hear fire sirens blaring. They wouldn't stop. Fire trucks and police cars joined in the cacophony, and though I went to the street and looked to the sky for smoke, I couldn't see any reason for such alarm. Later my father came grinning down the sidewalk from Main Street.

"What in the world was that?" I called out.

"Well," he started to speak, but he couldn't stop smiling. Finally he said, "It was Jimmie Blake's 75th birthday, and the firemen had a big party for him with a cake and everything. And they gave him a fireman hat and took him for a ride all up and down Main Street and around the library park, making all the noise they could with the sirens. He looked like he was having the time of his life."

I'm not quite sure just when he died, but he rated a front

page story in the weekly paper. Some time later a statue of John James Audubon was erected in the library park, and for fundraising purposes the city sold bricks with names engraved in them and placed them in a circular path all the way around the statue.

I bought a brick for Don Cole, the old bee man, and one for Jimmie Blake.

Proprieties

After thinking about it for a day or two I phoned Mr. Joseph. I was curious to meet him because he had worked in theater in Germany prior to World War II, but I was reluctant because I knew he was in his eighties. Allowing oneself to become fond of eighty-year-olds has its downside.

Curiosity won out.

His address led me into Montecito, a Santa Barbara suburb of wealthy estates scattered among a forest of grey-green valley oaks and a few less prepossessing homes. Mr. Joseph lived in an apartment newly built over a two-car garage next to an older, long-lived-in house.

I found the door to the stairway and pushed a buzzer button. A muffled but precise voice from above called out, "Please come in, Miss Sutcliffe," so I pushed open the door and started up the stairs.

At the top stood, unsteadily, a tall man with white hair combed neatly back from his face, piercing eyes, and aquiline nose. He took a slight, limping step toward me, bowed slightly, and extended a large, manicured hand. I put my smaller hand in his, and he held it for a long moment.

"Che gelida manina," he said.

Well, it was what passes for winter in southern California, and my hand, for one reason or another, was cool. I knew what he had said, because I had been going to an adult ed opera class, and we had watched films of *La Boheme*.

If you just say it in English, "What a cold hand," it comes off rather crass. But in Italian, at least when Rudolfo and Mimi first meet, it's more like, "Oh, what a dear, sweet, little cold hand you've got, let me warm it."

Mr. Rudolf Joseph did not release my little cold hand immediately. In fact, he applied to it a thoroughly Germanic hand kiss. Thus I understood quickly that he was sporting a set of false teeth that didn't fit terribly well. I extracted my hand.

He retreated to an armchair not far behind him, falling heavily into it. He motioned me to a nearby chair. A little side table sat between us.

"Would you care for some Asti Spumante?" he asked, proffering me a small stemmed glass. I would. Also on the little table he had a thick slice of Jarlsberg cheese and a knife. "A piece of cheese?"

"So, did you know Norbert Schiller?" I asked, nibbling the cheese. "He died just recently. You were both in the theater, I was told."

"I only knew him slightly," he said. "I grew up in Frankfurt, where he often performed. He was a little older than me. Things moved quickly in those days between the wars, and I became an assistant producer in Berlin in my early twenties. I brought Norbert to Berlin for a play I was working on. I had hoped to meet him again here in Santa Barbara. But we never quite got together."

Mr. Joseph had only been in Montecito for a year or so. "But I lived here in the fifties, after the war," he said, "and helped set up the filmmaking division for Brooks Institute. Then I was offered the opportunity to create an International Film Museum in Munich, so I returned to Europe. It was a wonderful time."

He paused and I saw his broad chest fill and release a silent sigh. "The actress I had loved for many, many years was finally free to be with me. We shared many good years. But after she died, I couldn't stand to see the places where we had been together, especially Italy, and I moved back to Montecito, because I had been happy here."

He asked me how I'd happened to know Norbert. "My ears always turn toward German, though I don't speak it very well myself," I said. "His voice drew me."

"When I was in high school," I elaborated. "I decided to become an intellectual. I stopped playing Elvis records. I wanted classical music, but I didn't know any. One day in a hardware store in Atlantic, Iowa, I found a small bin of LPs with pretty pictures on the covers. I found one with a goat-legged satyr and a fleeing nymph. It was by Debussy. I vaguely recognized him as a classical composer. I bought it.

"At home, on my Sears & Roebuck record player, I tried it out and was very disappointed. Classical, to me, meant orchestra. Instead, it was just a woman singing in a foreign language along with a piano. It was French on one side and German on the other. Debussy and Hugo Wolf. The voice and music began to intrigue me. I was especially drawn to the German side because the words were distinct. The French all ran together. There was an English translation of the songs on the album, but the original French and German were not included. I tried writing down the words of one German song, phonetically, and attempted to find them in a German dictionary at the public library. Not much luck.

"The next time I was at a store that sold records, I found one with Hans Hotter singing Schubert lieder, and all the German words were with it. I just continued on down that path. And Norbert—and you—I met along the way."

In further conversation, Mr. Joseph told me that he had fallen into depression when he first moved back to Montecito. He took a medley of complaints to his doctor, who said, "There's nothing wrong with you. You just need stimulation."

"So I started putting little want ads at the community college," he smiled. "I'd ask for students who would like to cook occasional meals for an elderly gentleman. I had to say 'students' but I never hired the boys, just the girls. At first the girls would be a little wary of me, but I never touched them.

I just enjoyed their bright and youthful spirits. They buoyed me up. I love to listen to them chatter about their schoolwork and boyfriends, and I'm like a grandfather to them."

"How many have you got?" I wondered.

"Oh, I have a calendar and I keep quite a schedule on it with about six different young women. It's like a production schedule for me. I enjoy keeping track of all of them and when they're scheduled to come cook for me. I don't care if they can't cook, you know. That's not why I pay them. I always have salmon and cheese anyway.

"But none of them speak any German or care about Schubert or Wolf or Puccini," he said, leaning slightly toward me.

He reached out and softly lifted a strand of my long hair that had fallen, as usual, across my face. My hair was very fine and never stayed pinned up for long.

I jumped, startled.

He sat back in his chair, a slight smile playing at the corners of his mouth.

"Ah," he said. "I see we must maintain some proper distance, Miss Sutcliffe."

"Yes, Mr. Joseph, I believe so," I answered, masking my own set of smiles within a lightly Victorian formality.

We spent almost every Wednesday evening together with Asti Spumante and Jarlsberg cheese for the next several years. We never stooped to using our first names.

One evening, as I started up the stairs, I heard the voice

of one of his flock of pretty students. "Bye, Rudy!" she called as she dashed down and past me.

And my first shocked thought was, "Such impropriety!"

Skin

THAT WONDERFUL NIGHT that Barack Obama so royally won. The enormous crowd pressing body to body and edge to edge in Chicago's Grant Park. I watched Obama's speech on my laptop in my Wisconsin kitchen, scanning the faces that the camera seized. I was looking for one face. If he is still alive in Chicago, he would have been there.

I never took part in any of the civil rights marches during those exciting years of the 1960s in Chicago. But Adolph Mathews and I stood together on the sidewalk cheering them on. We made our own quiet black and white statement wherever we went in those days.

My apartment was just two or three blocks from the south end of Lincoln Park. Not long after I moved to Chicago after graduating from college in Iowa, I had ventured out to a bar party with people I hardly knew. I was shy and curious. The Old Town area I lived in was lively. A jukebox was playing, and young people were dancing. I looked around for someone to dance with and noticed rather quickly the only black man in the place. He was older than most, had short, black, wavy hair combed backward, and a small moustache under a slightly concave nose. He wore a soft, rust-colored, cardigan sweater, and there was a pleasant roundness to the circumferences of his body.

My small town Midwest upbringing rarely brought me into close contact with black people. Very few.

I watched him dance with two different women. He caught my eyes on him, smiled, and then several times as he turned in the dance, his large brown eyes met mine. The dance over, he strolled to where I was sitting alone at a table.

"How about it?" he said, holding out a beautiful pink palm to me. I rose to him, and, a slow waltz starting, he pulled me close to his warm and sweet-smelling body, re-laxed and comfortable. We exchanged names during the dance. His was Adolph.

"Hell, no, I wasn't named for Hitler. In fact, I fought against the Nazis in World War II," he said. Pressed near to him, I could see freckles on his cheeks and nose amid the pleasant coffee color of his skin.

"I lied about my age. Enlisted when I was just 16, a pure patriot. I wanted to fight for my country. My family in Houston had been very protective of me as a child. Would you believe I never heard the word 'nigger' until a soldier on the base called me that? I learned a lot in the service. Grew up real fast."

The music changed to a jazzier beat, and Adolph just stepped along a bit quicker, rather than moving into swing mode. He looked down at me. "I just want you to know," he said, as he bopped up and down, "that not all black folk got rhythm."

We left the party bar and meandered down the Old Town streets, full of cafes, bars, and a somewhat diverse mix of peoples. "This is one of the few areas in Chicago that's sort of integrated," he told me. "It's a very segregated city." I didn't have a car and never traveled anywhere but between my apartment, Lincoln Park, and downtown, so I didn't know much about who lived where.

But I liked Adolph. His apartment was just two or three blocks from mine. He had a beautiful white Samoyed dog, which he walked frequently along the Old Town streets. And not just for the dog's sake. "People stop and talk to my dog," he confided. "They don't know how to just open up, but they ask me about the dog, and eventually they're talking to me. I make friends. I meet women. I have a good time."

He was the manager of a small dry cleaning factory owned by a Jewish man. "One day," Adolph said, "he was railing on and on about these lazy, stupid, good-for-nothing Negroes, and I stopped him and said, 'But I'm a Negro,' and you know what he said? 'Oh, but Adolph, you're different!'"

One night we were sitting on bar stools around a U-shaped little glass-topped bar, with tiny sprinkles of lights above it, wrapped around gold and silver metal leaves. I was listening closely to him, amid the bar noise, as he was telling me about a rich young white woman in Houston who picked him up on the street one time in her convertible, and took him home to bed, when he was very young. "It took me a little while," he said, "to realize that the reason she invited me to her home several times was just for sex. I thought there was friendship at first. I was wrong. It was just sexual thrills."

He paused for a moment and straightened slightly. Then, with one hand in front of his mouth, he looked down into his drink and said, in a low voice, "If you want to see a face of absolute hatred, look to the left behind you, but don't just turn around suddenly."

I stirred my drink with a straw, looked up at the lights, scratched my neck, yawned, and hoping I wasn't being too obvious, cast a glance to my left and back. A man, a white man, was hunched over his drink and staring at Adolph and me with nasty, narrowed eyes and a thin, set mouth.

"Did you ever see *Eros* magazine?" Adolph asked. "I'll show you a copy. It was a very beautiful, sophisticated magazine with a hard cover. Lots of photography and articles, stories, on the subject of love. Then they ran some little pictures of a black man kissing a white woman. They got put out of business by the post office. Censorship."

We left the bar, my coat pulled tightly around me. I don't know how he did it, but Adolph made women feel beautiful. It was partly the warmth of his appreciative glance and a few choice phrases, but more than that, it was a radiating beneficence and worldly good humor that gently caressed the objects of his affection.

He stepped into the street to hail a cab, and I was just a step behind him. As the empty cab hurtled on without even slowing, I saw the little muscle in Adolph's jaw clench.

We walked through the windy night to his apartment. It was small, just a bedroom, living room, bathroom, in an old building. I thought the bathroom was a bit of a shambles, with lots of spray bottles, jars of this and that, and a bit dusty. It needed a good cleaning, and I made a stupid comment about that.

"I'll have you know," Adolph said, "that I have been in a great many big, fancy bathrooms in big, fancy, rich houses. And I can tell you from experience that too many of those folks have really clean bathrooms but they are not personally clean. My bathroom may be a mess, but I shower twice a day, and I am always clean."

I backed off that subject really quick.

I loved looking at his bare body. It was a richness of hues and shadings. He took me by the hand and over many hours and days of talking in bed and in bars, he peeled away my small town innocence. It was a sexually adventurous time. The little pink pills in pink plastic cases made it possible. I was an independent, self-sufficient woman, and I wanted to know what men knew. Adolph was my teacher.

But I made one mistake. One afternoon we were in my

apartment, which had more space than furniture. We were playing around in our naked selves, and Adolph, laughing, picked me up, threw me gently over his shoulder, and spun the two of us around in circles. Then I noticed something, a small round scar on his lower back. I asked what it was. He lowered me to the floor and showed me a matching little round scar on his stomach.

"When I got out of the service, I was working, and I had some money. I bought a used Lincoln Continental. It was one handsome car. One day in Houston I drove into a shopping area and parked the car. This middle-aged white guy came out of a store, and he stopped in front of me. He says something like, 'Hey, boy, what's a nigger like you doin' with a nice car like that?' And something in me just exploded. Here I'd nearly gotten myself killed in the war, and this guy I was fighting for talks to me like that. I hit him, and we got into a knock down fight. I grabbed my gun from the glove compartment and I was going to beat him with it, I was just livid, and the gun went off. Didn't kill him, but I landed in prison for it pretty quick.

"I was in prison for over a year and a half, while my family were trying to get me out. I was in a work gang that did clean up work around logging operations in the woods. The foreman really didn't like me, and I was really careful not to be left alone with him. The other guys had warned me. But one day we were about to leave the work area, and the foreman hollers to me to go back and pick up an axe he'd left.

I turned around to go get it and realized everyone else was gone to the truck, and I'd just cooked my goose. I turned around with the axe in hand, and that foreman on his horse shot me. Right here," he said, putting my hand on the little round scar on his belly.

"The bullet went right through me, and I fell. I figured the only chance I had was to look dead, and that was what I did. He got off his horse and kicked me a couple times, then he left.

"I lay there for a long time, trying to stop the bleeding. It seemed like hours, but finally the foreman and the only guard who was halfway decent returned. The guard kicked me, said, 'You dead, Mathews?' And I was still alive.

"So they put me in the truck they had and drove me to a hospital, but they took the longest, slowest, roughest way around to get there. But I was still alive and I stayed awake.

"I recovered. I knew the foreman was afraid I'd tell how I got shot, but I kept my mouth shut. And after that he pretty much left me alone. Finally my family got me out."

I thought this was all so interesting that I wrote my parents about it. Mistake. My father and mother had never told me what to do about any aspect of my life. They always trusted I'd figure out what was best. Or, if they did attempt to influence me, it was pretty subtle and done through stories of what happened in their lives due to choices made. My dad had only spanked me once when I was little, and that was because I sassed him. I was a good girl and didn't get in trouble. So here I was having adventures in the big city, and I wrote home about how Adolph got his matching scars. I got a letter back from my father, who normally left writing to my mother. It was handwritten, and he told me briefly and firmly to end my relationship with Adolph immediately. "That fellow is taking advantage of you."

I considered this and decided he was wrong, but only from my perspective. I stopped applying my journalistic talents to letters home and instead kept the subject matter limited to weather, work, and interesting recipes.

So my parents never heard my Billie Holiday records, nor knew how much I adored the inimitable voice Adolph introduced me to. At one time he had lived in the same apartment house as Billie. "She always fell in love with the goddamnedest sons of bitches," he said, shaking his head in dismay.

I didn't tell them that we'd been in a bar one night in Old Town when Dizzie Gillespie played. That I actually drank a beer now and then.

Gradually Adolph and I drifted on into other love affairs. He introduced me to a small, lovely black woman of whom he was very protective. She had been much abused as a child. They intended to marry.

I left for Germany in 1967 and returned to Iowa in 1968 to start up a small pottery business in my western Iowa hometown. I lived with my parents for the first year. One day my father handed me the phone with a strange look. It was

Adolph. He and his wife would be driving through Iowa on their way west, and they'd head up Hiway 71 to Audubon if I'd like to have lunch with them. "Oh, sure," I said. "We can go to the Holiday Cafe on the highway at the edge of town. Pick me up at the house."

My father's face was unknowable. "You can't go out to a public place with them," he said. "Mom will fix lunch for us all right here. And that's that."

Adolph and his wife came. We all sat around the kitchen table and tried to eat and tried to talk, but the atmosphere was stiff and solemn. I felt cold and paralyzed. Adolph and his wife thanked my parents politely and went on their way. My parents said nothing further.

If I had the power to remake anything in my life, it would be that day.

Legacy of Edward Fitzgerald

H E WAS A DECENT ENOUGH DANCER, not great, but decent. And better than no partner at all. So we went to the Saturday night dances at the Rec Center in Santa Barbara for a few weeks, arm in arm.

I don't remember his name. And he wasn't much for conversation. He was stocky and strong, his grey hair butch cut. He knew the basic ballroom steps and didn't experiment with them. He thought he was a good dancer because he'd taken some Arthur Murray lessons, and I didn't discourage him, because he'd told me his wife had left him and he was out dancing to keep his spirits up.

But the real reason I kept on dancing with him was because of something else he'd told me. After his wife left him, his house in Thousand Oaks burned down. And he was a firefighter by trade, and he couldn't save his own house.

That made me feel sorry for him, but that still wouldn't have kept me following such an unimaginative dancer in basic box waltz patterns around the ballroom floor for weeks when there were a lot better and more creative dancers on the hoof.

It was the other thing he'd said.

"I was really depressed," he told me. "After my wife left me and the fire took the house, I was really really down, and I didn't know what to do or where to turn. And my brother said, 'Why don't you read *The Rubaiyat of Omar Khayyam*?'

"So I went to a bookstore and bought a copy and read it. Everything in it was just how life is. You can't change a thing."

He closed his eyes and quoted:

"The Moving Finger writes and having writ,

Moves on. Nor all thy Piety nor Wit

Shall lure it back to cancel half a Line,

Nor all thy Tears wash out a Word of it.

"It helped me think straight," he said. "I read it over and over and over until I memorized the whole damn thing."

And I—I was an English major.

The Embrace

THE FIRST TIME Norbert Schiller came to my house in Santa Barbara for supper, I worried over how to cook for a gaunt 82-year-old who had been a strict vegetarian since he was 21 and a heartthrob on the German stage. His wife, much younger than he, was an expert at it, flavoring grains, beans, and vegetables with herbs such as thyme and Hungarian paprika in combinations foreign to me. But she was happy to have a night off and merrily dropped Norbert at my gate.

Baked potatoes were within my aura of competence.

Norbert lavished the buttered bundles with succulent praise. He enjoyed food and was no sophisticated and fussy gourmet. We sat at the little round table in my combination dining nook and living room, talking about poetry and theater, paying no heed to the graying, sculptured yellow carpet that I couldn't afford to replace. After the strawberries and ice cream appeared, Norbert ascended into even higher evocations of praise and appreciation, quite genuine, as they were blended with his delight in our recently formed friendship.

And then, as I was starting to remove the dishes from the table, he stood up.

He was about my height, though slightly bowed, a thin and wiry man, with an unruly shock of bountiful grey hair and a profound moustache and noble nose. In a sudden move, he wrapped his arms tightly around me, and I found my mouth entangled with his moustache in a moment of—to me—great confusion.

A moment sometimes can last a very long time. This one threw me into a flashing revisit to a haunting exhibit of huge drawings on butcher paper by the printmaker and University of Iowa art professor Mauricio Lasansky. I had seen these pieces many years ago in Iowa City. They were called *The Nazi Drawings*. They appeared to have been sketched rapidly in a terrible passion of remembrance, horror, and pity. The nearly lifesize images showed, over and over, in varying emphases, German military, civilians, and priests, embraced by skeletal figures whose heads were like battle helmets with teeth. The arms and legs of the skeletons began to blend with the living as the evil consumed them. Once seen, these drawings can never be forgotten.

Being suddenly and tightly enfolded by a German Jew who had escaped the Nazis redrew those frightening images around me. Norbert's strong thin arms were too much like the boney skeleton lurking still alive beneath his freckled skin. I felt in that moment embraced by Death.

But then the moustache tickled me. I remembered that Norbert was still very much alive and that he was clutching me with perhaps the last passion of his years. He had always been a romantic man, dallying with stage actresses during the heady years between wars. He didn't marry until he was forty-five and living alone with goats in a stone cabin in the Ojai outback. Mary was vegetarian and could cook, and she was a lovely little dark-haired, dark-eyed sprite. When she first moved to Ojai a friend said, "There are just two fascinating men in Ojai, Krishnamurti and Norbert Schiller." Mary went after Norbert.

She was never jealous of his roving eye. On an extended trip alone to Europe, she cut her expenses considerably by staying with a network of former Norbertian lovers, giving each one Norbert's greetings and remembrance. She had a fine time.

So I didn't panic, and I didn't push away. I cannot truthfully say that I enjoyed that embrace, but I did understand its loving intent. And it demanded a follow through the next time that Mary wanted an evening off to drive to Los Angeles for an Anthroposophical meeting.

Norbert came equipped that night. He brought with him two beeswax candle stubs to burn for the occasion, and a handful of violets. "They remind me," he said, "of the cyclamen that grew wild in the Vienna Woods, when I was a boy."

I spread out a comforter on the yellow carpet, and Norbert put his candles on either side, on little dishes, and lit them. I turned out the lights. The evening air was sweet-scented, drifting in through open french doors to the little backyard with a small orange tree, a mature avocado, and a high honeysuckle hedge.

We took off our clothes. Menopause and gravity had not grasped me yet. I was still lithe and slim, with, as another gentleman once put it, "that pale English skin." Norbert was very thin, and there was hardly enough freckled flesh on him to sag. He was mostly bone and remembrance. I attempted to resurrect some semblance of former glory to the small, limp bud at his groin, without success. But we embraced, body to body, which was enough, and the old romantic whispered to me, "When I lie in your arms, I forget Vienna."

It did not seem necessary to repeat that evening, but it had deepened our feeling for one another. And my under-standing of aging.

The next day I was downtown near the Lobero Theater and happened to notice an old man walking slowly along the sidewalk. He was like a dark silhouette of faded life, and I realized that, normally, I would never have noticed him at all. He would have been a shadow passing. Invisible. Now I looked at this man and wondered whom he had loved and whom he still might love. And did anyone still love him? Could he be, like Norbert, a young and romantic man wear-ing the ill-fitting costume of too many years?

More than once after Norbert's death, Mary said to me,

"You know, Norbert really loved you. I'm so happy that you were his friend, 'cause you could talk to him about poetry. He loved all that, you know."

Norbert Schiller in one of his romantic roles on the German stage.

Capra Press

I MADE FRIENDS one summer with a woman who had the biggest and most eclectic book collection I'd ever seen. Her wandering rooms in Santa Barbara, not far from the ocean, were full of bookcases, floor to ceiling, full of a fascinating collection of everything from coffee table art books to all of Gertrude Bell's travel books of the desert. Frances Holden told me one time that she simply gave up on getting carpenters to build bookcases the way she wanted, so she'd just built many of them herself. In her late 80s, when I knew her, she always hoped that an earthquake would bury her under her books, her idea of the perfect demise. We both loved books and had a similar passion for acquisition, though Frances totally surpassed my capabilities of both finance and storage.

Gradually I realized that she had lived in that house since the 1940s with someone famous, a German opera star, Lotte Lehmann, who had died in 1976. The centennial of her birth was approaching in 1988, and UCSB library potentates were trying to stir up a mild celebration, a resurrection on a shoestring. An opera professor from the University of Iowa, Beaumont Glass, volunteered to write a biography of the singer, and for several months Beau bunked and boarded at Frances' house. He would descend the stairs in the morning in a long, gold brocade housecoat and slippers, his long white hair swept back, and he and Frances would discuss the next chapter's details. She, much less gallantly attired and far less handsome, was the fount of authorized accuracy. Beau had been one of Lotte's pianists at the Music Academy of the West, which she and Frances founded during their retirement years. But it was Frances who knew everything about Lotte and protected Lotte.

I saw a problem approaching.

It was the summer of 1987, and if they were going to get a biography published for 1988, they were way, way behind schedule. How many publishers would they have to contact to find one who'd accept a biography of a dead soprano? Audience limited.

"Frances," I said, after explaining to her the timing problem, "I know a way to solve this. I know Noel Young, the publisher of Capra Press, here in Santa Barbara. I also know that he will sometimes publish a worthy book if someone pays for the printing costs. If you'd put up the money, I'll bet he'd publish the biography. And you'd have it in time for the centennial."

"You're probably right," she muttered, brows knitted. Her short, almost white, grey hair stood up in unkempt peaks above her stalwart face. She was sitting on an old flowered couch in the garden room, with almost as many pots of plants inside the glass doors as outside in the surrounding patio. A parrot perched in a cage, its feather coat threadbare. A mangy, smelly old spaniel lay beside Frances. Its tail had cancerous lumps hanging from it, a very disgusting sight. But that old hound was the last of the many dogs that Frances and Lotte had owned and loved together, and I figured out really quick that no complaints were to be made, no noses wrinkled.

"But don't tell Beau about this," said Frances. "I don't want him to know I'm paying for his book."

Capra Press was often referred to as "legendary." It was one of the few small California presses that managed to survive quite a few years by printing a variety of books, mostly literary but with some intriguing potboilers that paid off. The big one for Noel was a book on hot tubs, which included many photos of his friends, young, potted, and, especially, nubile, cavorting around a whole hillside of homemade hot tubs. That book put him in business.

It also gave him an erotic reputation that, in the later years that I knew him, was a little hard for him to keep up. Though he gave it a good try. Our shift into platonic friendship was quick. He was small and slim, with fine gray hair, and with a mild look of gentle dishevelment about him, no matter what he was wearing.

When I met him, at the first annual book fair in Santa

Barbara, he still owned a printing press, though his books were being printed elsewhere. He showed me the press one day, and he gave me some colorful broadsides he had printed from metal type and woodcuts, Edward Lear nonsense verses.

"Far and few, far and few, are the lands where the Jumblies live," he read from one of the large, thick sheets, "Their heads were green and their hands were blue, and they went to sea in a sieve.

"It's a lot like publishing," he said, with a faint smile. "I miss having ink on my hands." But book publishing needed faster technology if it was to support his wife and young daughter, his second family.

They lived in a handmade house perched over the Santa Barbara River valley. It was round and had a huge stone fireplace in the center that supported rafters like spokes radiating from a wheel hub. Noel had built the fireplace. He had learned stonework somewhere in his life. He'd met Henry Miller while building a stone wall for him, and later he published some of Miller's smaller works.

Capra means goat. Noel was a Capricorn, as was I. I found a small carved stone goat head for him, and he mortared it into a niche in the expansive fireplace. It was easy to ask Noel to take on the Lehmann biography. It would be a prestigious book for his press to publish. Just not a moneymaker, aside from sales to a coterie of Lehmannites around the world.

Noel accompanied me to Frances' Hope Ranch home. Frances, her eyes bright with possibility, was waiting in the garden room with the old dog. When Noel expressed interest in the house, she took him for a tour. She walked very straight-backed, taking small, careful steps with her little feet in sensible shoes. The dog shambled after her, its ugly tail swinging. Noel was shown Lotte's baby grand piano and on top of it the clay bas relief of Toscanini she had made of her great friend and, possibly, lover. When he died, Lotte had thrown his letters into the fireplace to burn but couldn't bear to light the match. Frances had rescued them and stuffed them behind a file cabinet, forgotten until the book project.

Noel was pleased with the idea of the book and the up front cash that would pay the printing costs. It was a good bargain for both him and Frances. She was much relieved that the book could be completed in time for the centennial celebration. And she was pleased that Beau would know nothing of the financial transaction making it possible.

As we left the house, strolling under the bougainvillea that cascaded from roofs and trees around the patio, Noel said, "Old houses in England in the old days must have smelled like that. . . ."

As a thank you to me, Noel asked me to design the book and to use one of the computer fonts I had designed. He also requested that my friend Roger Levenson, knowledgeable in both music and book arts, edit the book. Roger and I came free, of course, but probably worked three times as hard as if we were being paid.

The great crisis arrived when Noel told us that Beau's nearly finished manuscript was too long, and that thirty-two pages needed to be cut. Roger bared his sword, and we went at it, slashing out what Roger considered an excess of gushy quotes from newspaper critics scattered all the way through the book. "Two is enough for this Carnegie concert," Roger would say. "Scratch out the rest. What does Beau think he's doing, larding it up with six quotes? He's putting in every superlative any critic ever wrote. Enough already."

Then there was the language. Beau tended to sweeten sentences with overdone words like "lovely" and "exquisite." Roger would grumble and grump and cross out the excess effervescence with his red pencil.

The edited manuscript was sent to Beau, back in Iowa City, chapter by chapter, as we worked. The pages would return with an angry huff of scribbles in the margins, "Put that back!! This is MY STYLE!!! You're ruining the book!"

"I'm glad you're handling this," Noel said to me, shaking his head, as he read the rages on the returned manuscripts. Roger and I, now stolid professionals, continued with the red pencils. Beau got madder and madder and insisted we were mangling his book. The truth was that the book was much improved by being tightened up, with a little more restraint in the language.

Things finally came to a showdown. Beau handed in a

chapter near the end of the book in which it appeared as if Lotte, late in life, looking towards death, might have taken up religion in the form of Anthroposophism, an esoteric philosophy based on the writings of Rudolf Steiner, of which Beau, and, apparently, the late conductor Bruno Walter, were enamored. Beau's theory was based on one letter from Lotte to Bruno.

When Frances read that chapter, she blew up, like a little steam engine, huffing and puffing. "Lotte was just being nice. She didn't give a damn about religion. She was being kind to Bruno. Her religion was nature. I refuse to let Beau print that chapter. It has to change. I've tried to keep out of this, but if he won't back down and change that chapter, I'll have to do something grim."

It came down to that. I had phoned Noel to say that Frances was adamant that Beau had to change that chapter and accept the edits. But she refused to be the one to tell him. I was the middleman. "Noel, you've got to call him," I pleaded. Noel was not happy about confrontations and put it off as long as he could.

The day finally came. I sat across the desk from Noel in his office, with books, manuscripts and coffee cups stacked on shelves, on tables, on chairs, on his desk. Photos and drawings of goats were pinned in any open spaces on the walls. He cleared the desktop in front of him and sat the telephone there. He stared at it.

"I'm nervous," he said. "I've never had a writer act like

this before. They're always so thrilled to be published, they are just grateful. And they are happy to have good editing. That's the sign of a real professional, they want good editing. They know its value." He sighed and took a deep breath. "Well. Here goes."

He took a slug of coffee, and dialed up Beau in Iowa City. He first tried to reason with him, but that didn't get very far. Beau on the other end was obstinate, his heels dug in deep. No changes.

"I wish I didn't have to tell you this," Noel wavered, looking at me and gritting his teeth. "But I guess I have to. The book will not be printed if the cuts and editing are not made and if the chapter on religion is not changed to reflect Frances' wishes. Frances is paying for the publishing of this book. If you want the book to go forward, you will have to... to go along with her wishes."

That was that. "I'm exhausted," sighed Noel. "I'm heading down the street for a beer."

The book, tidied up, turned out well. The centennial was better than expected. Some books were sold. The rest may still be sitting in a warehouse for all I know. I have two copies, one signed by Frances, Noel, and Roger.

Noel always had an aura of sweet forgetfulness about him, absent-minded in a gentle way. It gradually developed into Alzheimers in the years after I moved from Santa Barbara. His wife left him. I received a couple letters from friends who were organizing fund raising to help care for him. Eventually the notice of his death arrived, and then a newspaper clipping about the purchase of Capra Press by a bookseller. There is a Capra Press website, but I'm not sure that it's active. Links go to university library collections of Capra's output. Under "History," however, is a picture of Noel Young in his hot tub.

Willie Craig swing dancing in Ventura, in his late 70s or early 80s.

His Fantasy

Should I drive down to the Ventura Harbor and look for him? Or not? I didn't know anything about him, except that he lived on a boat, and I'd danced half the night with him at the Santa Barbara Rec Center's Friday night ballroom dance. A black Greek fisherman's cap topped his head, haloed by a tangle of reddish gray curls. His blue eyes were mischievous, his smile broad. There was a slight bow to the legs. He was a challenge of a dancer. He followed no regular dance patterns, but lead me so well, in such perfect rhythm, that I easily followed his innovative swoops and whirls around the light-dappled floor.

Something about him drew me.

And there in front of me was his sailboat, perched upright in dry dock, a 30 ft. long, light blue, old, fiberglas tub. Willie was painting a stripe around the darker blue bottom. He turned toward my footsteps, blinking in the sunshine, and augmented his cap's brim with his hand.

"You surprised me," he said with a grin. "I really didn't think you'd take me up on the invite."

"I was curious," I said. "There aren't many sailboats in Iowa, where I come from. Nor sailors who dance well. I enjoyed dancing with you."

"Me, too," he said. "Come enter my parlor and have a cup of tea. I'm ready to sit down for a bit." He motioned to a ladder leaning against the boat's railing. He scampered up first, turned, and bent down to steady my hand as I climbed over the rail.

The deck looked old but cleanly scraped. "I bought it for $5,000," he said, demonstrating how to turn and climb down a short ladder into the cavity of the boat, facing the ladder rather than the interior. "Got to learn the safe ways and stick to them," he said. "Otherwise when there's an emergency, you forget how to do it right, and you mess up. You don't usually get a second chance on the ocean.

"She was built in 1968. She's solid. Just slow. I threw everything inside of it out. Including the stinky indoor toilet and the old gas engine. I just put in a little diesel motor a few days ago."

He turned on a gas jet of a two-burner stove that appeared able to rock with the swells of the sea. He made tea for us in a couple unmatched mugs decorated with advertising. Tossed a few packets of restaurant saltines on the table.

"I'm always putting them in my pocket at Denny's. They help keep sea sickness at bay. That and looking at the horizon. Want to come sailing with me when I get this rig in the water?"

"Might," I said. "You actually live here?"

"Sure," he answered, removing his cap and combing his graying curls with his strong fingers. "I don't need much room. And I can live on next to nothing. Social security and a little money left in savings. I have stuff, though, tools and clothes and all. I like garage sales. I rent a storage unit for all that."

He'd been sailing since he was a kid on Staten Island. "My father taught my older sister how to sail. But he wouldn't bother to teach me, thought I was too dumb to learn," he said, cornering transparent bits of cracker packaging under one hand.

"I just borrowed the boat when nobody was around and taught myself. Trial and error. That's how I've had to learn most everything."

He'd taught himself dancing as well. His eyes lit up as he explained, "Yeah, I learned to dance by skipping school and sneaking off to Times Square. I loved those big bands. I watched people dancing, and I imitated them, and that's how I learned to dance. But I have to do it my own way. All that counting and left, right, do si do mixes me all up."

Tea and tour finished, I started to make my goodbyes, but he grabbed me by the ladder, pushing me back against it, and gave me a fairly lascivious kiss, a close relative of the one in the hibiscus bush with which we'd ended the ballroom dance the night before.

"Come to the dance next Friday night?" he whispered.

"I wouldn't miss it."

We danced almost every dance during the first half of the night. I was getting a few mildly envious looks from some of the older dancing ladies in their chiffons, high heels, and spray net. I was in a black skirt and top with low-heeled black sandals, hair drifting loose below my shoulders. Willie's hands on me were warm and intimate, lightly but firmly guiding me wherever he wanted us to go.

During the long intermission, instead of eating cake and Kool-Aid, we went up into the darkened balcony. It was hot, and windows up there were open. Willie sat on the ledge of one of them. He pulled me between his legs, and we experimented with more kissing. It was very hot.

"I have a fantasy," he said, his eyes half closed. "It's been with me a long time. I kidnap a woman, usually a hitchhiker, and take her home with me where I tie her up in the cellar and force her to do whatever I want."

"Oops," I thought to myself. "What have I got here?"

"I make her do what I want," he continued softly. "I make her read to me. I make her have sex in every possible way. If she refuses I punish her. I can go through this same fantasy with every different woman in *Playboy*."

His eyes were closed, and the evening breeze rippled the folds of his shirt.

I'm not afraid of fantasies. Usually, that's all they are. And I'd heard the key to Willie Craig.

"What do you have her read to you?" I asked, my fingers lightly tangling in his curls.

"Stories," he said. "Anything I want to know about."

He reached out to take my head in his hands and kiss me gently.

"Can we make the woman in the fantasy read to us?" I breathed.

"Sure, she'll do anything we want her to."

Over the next few days, months, and years, I learned more deeply what it was like to be dyslexic, and how painful.

Willie, born in 1925, had been dyslexic before anyone bandied that term about. "They always thought I was dumb in school because I couldn't read," he said. "But I always knew somehow that I was smartdumb. I could do other things, like sports, like sailing, better than the other kids. It just didn't make my report cards look any better.

"I never learned to read until I was drafted into the Navy," he went on. We were lying comfortably in bed in my house, my cat curled at our feet.

"My only real buddy on the ship to Okinawa was a Mexican kid. He was a carpenter like me. He taught me to say the alphabet in Spanish. I still say the letters like he did.

"It took me a long time to teach myself to read. It was hard, but I did it, and I did it well enough to struggle through the real estate exam so I could buy and sell houses in Orange County. I bought foreclosed houses, fixed them up, and re-sold them. Not easy. Sometimes I would sit up in bed in the middle of the night, worried sick about how I was going to take care of my family.

"But then my wife divorced me. After that, I just said to hell with it all, sold the houses I had left. Stopped working. I haven't worked for years. I have about $50,000 left in the bank. I just live cheap on $600 social security and a little every month from my savings account."

Willie liked to work on his boat during the week and come stay with me on weekends. I had to buy a white shirt so I could usher with him at the several live theaters in Santa Barbara. He'd been doing it for years and loved the musicals especially. We got in free if we ushered.

We were friends and lovers. He was always gentle and silly. He was great fun to talk with. There was always an equal give and take. I liked to ask him for advice on any subject because he thought at oblique angles, which oftentimes were very creative.

Once he got the old boat back in the sea, he'd take it out in a storm to a dangerous promontory, known for shipwrecks, to try out his current configuration of sails. He'd limp back to the harbor with sails in tatters, and try to figure out what was wrong. He reworked the whole sail design several times over before he was satisfied.

One day I came in the house to find him at my dining table hunched over my little Royal portable typewriter. "Feel my forehead," he said.

It was wet with cold perspiration. "This is how hard it

is for me to try to write," he said. "It is physically so difficult that I avoid doing it as much as possible."

I was onto my second Macintosh computer, so I put the little old original 1984 Mac in one of the bedrooms and told Willie he could play at typewriting on the little computer. I showed him a teach yourself typewriting game. It fascinated him, and he poked the keys in order to shoot down alphabet letters and combinations of letters as they fell down the screen. He began to spend a lot of time working with it. Gradually he gathered some speed and accuracy, and it made him more confident about trying to write.

Willie never read books for fun. Nothing about reading was fun. It was torture. It was possible, when necessary, but always painful. He wasn't interested in any kind of books. Nothing in print tempted him. Except, I noticed, the full color photos in National Geographic magazines, especially pictures of early man—and woman.

I bought Jean Auel's thick novel, *The Clan of the Cave Bear*.

"I've got this book, Willie," I proffered. "About a girl who's taken in by a tribe of Neanderthal cave men. Want to hear the first chapter? I'll read it to you." I sat down on the futon couch.

Willie stood next to me, swaying a bit impatiently from side to side. "I should be heading back to the boat," he said.

"Well, maybe I'll listen to just a little." He sat down on the couch.

I started reading about the plucky little girl who lost her mother and tribe in an earthquake and was raked across the thigh by a cave bear. There was plenty of immediate action. Willie drew closer to me. By the time the curious Neanderthal tribe found the poor little thing, Willie was nestled into my side like a little boy, totally enthralled.

One by one, over many months, I read all of the first four books in the series aloud to Willie. They were all thick, fat books. As long and detailed as the novels were, we never wanted them to end. I loved to read aloud, and he adored being read to. When we finished Book Number Four, we knew that there were two more books in the series that the author, Jean Auel, had promised but had not yet written.

In 1996 I sold my house in Santa Barbara and semi-retired to my hometown of Audubon, Iowa. At first, Willie said he would come with me, but when the day of decision actually arrived, he refused to go back to winter weather.

"I worked too hard to get a foothold in California, where it's warm. I can't leave it now. I don't like being cold."

That was a dozen years ago.

Willie is now 84. He sold the boat and bought an inexpensive mobile home in a seniors' rent-controlled park. His bank account has run out, but it doesn't seem to have made much difference. Social security and an abundance of free food for seniors keeps him going. He runs up and down the long steps to the beach several times a week. He doesn't drive the thirty miles to Santa Barbara dances much anymore, but he still goes dancing in Ventura.

And he writes me letters on a PC he bought for $10 at a garage sale. He took a computer class at the community college, using the still operative GI bill. He works occasionally on a little book about ballroom dancing secrets he's learned over the years. He explains how to sneak forbidden cornstarch onto the floor by your chair to rub your dancing shoe soles in. He gives tips on how to appeal to the ladies. It's a long term project.

From one of his recent letters: *"A great deal has been learned by me. Most of which I will never use. This is pattern for me, to get off to a slow start and then wiggle my way to learning things the hard way. I would venture to say that most people would not have the patience to keep at it for so long. I seem to be coming apart as someone my age should perhaps. My knee is a bit on the sore side but is getting well in the usual fashion for me. This has deprived me from dancing for the past month or so. Monday night I will give it a try at the Poinsettia Pavilion."*

Jean Auel eventually got around to publishing Book Number Five. I mailed a copy to Willie, and he read it himself. And I read it. And we talked about it on the phone.

We're still waiting for Book Number Six.

Myself and Roger Levenson in front of the tile plaque on the
Santa Barbara Courthouse exterior that I designed and painted
to honor Queen Elizabeth II 's visit to the city in 1983.

Ring Around

Duction the 1980s in Santa Barbara, I occasionally did
graphic work for Capra Press, one of California's legendary
small presses. Noel Young was publisher and everything else,
aided by his wife and a network of freelancers who were always happy to design, illustrate, edit, set type, or do whatever was needed to produce the ten to fifteen eclectic books
Noel published each year. Everyone, including Noel, did it
more for love than money.

In 1987 Noel asked me to design a book about Lotte
Lehmann that was being published to celebrate the 100th
anniversary of the German soprano's birth. She had lived for
many years in Santa Barbara and was instrumental in starting the Music Academy of the West.

Noel knew that I would do this for next to nothing just
to have the opportunity to try out my computer type de-
signs in a real typesetting project. It would be one of the
first books he published totally typeset on a little Macintosh
computer. My friend and mentor Roger Levenson was really

tickled when I got that job, and as Noel well knew, Roger, retired book arts lecturer at Berkeley, would be looking over my shoulder and making sure I did a professional job of setting up the book's front matter, the chapter headings, and the ending colophon where I could mention my font and the Mac.

The typesetting was the easy part.

There were also to be quite a few pages devoted to photographs. I was handed a box crammed with old publicity photos of Lotte Lehmann, dating from the early 1900s into the '60s. She had sung more than ninety different roles. I was to fit as many diverse photos as possible into three allotted photo sections. And write captions.

I ruffled through the pictures. They were a strange lot. In one of them, Lotte—I had to assume all the photos were of her— was dressed as a cave girl wrapped in furry skins, a bare and provocative shoulder showing. In another she took a holier-than-thou innocent maiden pose in a long gown. In the next she was attired in a heavily gold-encrusted oriental outfit with a huge, haughty head-dress. And then there was Lotte in a sturdy leather buccaneer outfit, boots to the hips. Who in the world were all these characters? On the back of the photos and photo postcards I'd find just the first names of girls penciled in. Elsa, Eva, Elizabeth, Agathe, Leonore, Sophie. The names muddled my head. How was I supposed to know who they were and what operas they were from?

Happily, my fountain of book arts knowledge, Roger Levenson, responded to my cry of "Help!"

He sat down with me at my dining room table, took off his beret, and smoothed his long and thinning grey hair. I spread out all the photos. Roger had never talked to me about opera before, as we were always involved in type and books. Now, having been asked, he did. He picked up the photo of the slightly plump woman wrapped in a bear skin and little else.

"Okay," he said, adjusting his bifocals. "You have to understand that I'm biased toward the Wagnerian side of things, despite my Jewish parentage. This one is Sieglinde. Lotte was one of opera's finest Sieglindes. Her performances with Melchior were hot. There were even complaints about her in this opera—*Die Valkyrie*. Some nincompoops fussed that she burned up the stage, she was way too sexy. But she just knew what was in that magnificent, passionate music. She was a natural."

He warmed to his subject. "You must know that Sieglinde was married to a real redneck of the woods, big cruel guy, but this other fellow—they all were running around in furs—shows up on her doorstep one night, and they immediately fall in love. What neither of them knows is that they are brother and sister, Siegmund and Sieglinde, violently separated as children. When they begin to figure that out and start singing about love and springtime, it's total passion."

He gave me a stern look. "Don't raise your eyebrows over the incest part. It's symbolic."

I lowered my brows and shut my mouth. He was on a roll. "If you listen to Lotte sing that aria, even on an old 78 rpm record, it will make the hair on your neck stand on end. That's what happens to me once in a great while in a live opera performance. One voice will send those chills down my back. Doesn't happen often, but when it does, you know why you put up with all the grand silliness that goes along with opera."

I was hoping he'd drop the sibling love affair and go on to Miss Leatherstocking's photo, but he was mesmerized by those bare shoulders.

"This is just the first act of *Die Valkyrie*. There are four operas in Wagner's Ring cycle. You have to understand that it's not just the story, it's the leitmotives that Wagner deals with. You see, he starts off the whole thing with music that sounds like the depths of the ocean except it's the Rhine with rising waters, undulating waves, and tittering mermaids, and from those water melodies are born many little signature melodies that permeate all four operas. There's a beautiful love motif for Sieglinde, for instance, and a heroic one for her brother and an evil one for her husband, and a noble one for the sword that's stuck in the tree, and a wildly lyrical one for springtime. Wagner weaves all this together as background for the story that's happening on stage, and the music tells you things the characters don't even know themselves...."

"You're looking vexed," he said.

"All I wanted to know was what opera Sieglinde was in," I said. "And how do you spell it? And does she have a last name, or do all these ladies just go by their first names?"

Roger examined my popcorn plaster ceiling for a moment, and then said, "Actually, I brought a book for you. The plots of all the major operas and all the main characters' names. If you scrounge around in it, I think you'll find out who all these mystery gals are. I could tell you, but it would be more fun for you to go hunting. Now, the important thing, where shall we go for dinner?"

I didn't know it just then, but he had hooked me. I sorted through the photos, looking up each of the names in the opera book and reading the stories. There was Lotte as Tosca, ready to murder the elegant villain with a fruit knife. There she was as stupid little Elsa who fell in love with a mysterious knight who ran away with a swan when she inquired after his name. And somehow nobody recognized that inside the leather tunic and hip boots was quite an ample, buxom woman, Lotte as Leonore.

By the time I had all the photos sorted out and captions written to show the broad reach of Lotte's opera career, I had pretty well completed Introduction to Opera 101.

But I only knew the names and the stories.

Next came the music. Roger and I were driving to Solvang one Saturday morning for Danish ableskiver and red raspberry jam, and he turned on the radio. "Hey, it's Wagner," he said. "*The Flying Dutchman.* Doomed sea captain meets innocent girl who throws herself into the ocean to redeem him. . . . Women are always so stupid. . . . This is where all the females are spinning. Hear those spinning wheels?"

He pulled the car off the road. We sat there oblivious of cars whizzing by us and listened to the rest of the Texaco broadcast. Roger directed the orchestra with his hands, above the steering wheel, and he kept up a running commentary on what was going on. "Here comes the death ship. Now wait, in a little bit, the cursed sea captain will appear...there, hear that theme? He's doomed. You'll hear it again."

We did a lot of driving on Saturdays after that, and every time he turned on the radio there seemed to be another opera in full glory. He loved to tell me what was happening on stage, and it didn't matter what language the story was in, he knew what was going on. And I began to find it fun.

"Now listen close, this will be fast," he admonished. "The Marschallin is in bed with a 17-year-old boy right there on stage, unless they've got a modesty curtain... there, he's going at it... whoop! whoop! whoop! Ooops. Drooping, drooping, done."

"How can they play such sexy stuff on the radio?" I asked, my eyes rather wide at what I'd just heard.

"Most people don't know what they're hearing," he laughed. "There are opera secrets. That's one. *Rosenkavalier.* There's another sexy moment in *Die Valkyrie* when Siegmund pulls the sword out of the tree and turns it toward Sieglinde. Well, if there was ever a phallic symbol, that's it."

"Hmmm," I contemplated. "Do you think Lotte knew that?"

"There are a lot of Sieglindes who cry out just then. They're no prudes. But you have to know these things. Gotta be aware."

The Lehmann book was finished and published. The centennial year was celebrated. Roger, feeling his years, moved back to San Francisco and bought into an assisted living place. He wanted to be near the San Francisco Opera. *The Ring* was coming.

"Now, listen," he said on the phone, "I will buy you tickets to go to *The Ring* with me. But only if you promise that you'll buy the Solti *Ring* on CDs and listen to all of it and study it really well before you ever come up here. I'll send you a book about the *Ring* leitmotives, and you should get familiar with them. Will you promise me to do that? You can't enjoy this if you don't study it first."

"Okay, Roger, I'll do it."

Those tickets were expensive for Roger, four nights of big whomping live opera for the two of us. The Solti CDs weren't cheap, either. But I bought them and listened carefully and tried to track the little melodies. I loved the nattering rhythms of the dwarves and their hammers, and the galumphing gait of the giants was easy to identify. The more I listened to the love themes, the deeper they invaded my heart.

We went to *The Ring* in style. I wore a long dress. Roger, I remember, was really decked out. I'd sewn for him by hand a vest made from several of his favorite silk neckties. A navy blue one had the letters RR all over it, meaning railroads, another of his eclectic interests. A burgundy one had the names of operas woven into it in gold. A blue and red striped one had little antique printing presses scattered across it. The three things he knew and loved best of all. He looked distinguished in his dark suit, with the richly colored vest and his black beret.

That was my first *Ring* cycle on stage, but it was Roger's thirteenth. And who knows how many times he had listened to it on records. I don't remember that San Francisco *Ring* very well, to tell the truth. After listening to CDs in solitude, having lots of people around me wiggling and coughing was very distracting. To this day I prefer opera canned or filmed. I do recall that the Sieglinde in San Francisco was tall and slim, blonde and pretty. She looked the part, but Roger grumbled afterward, "She didn't have the voice for it. Pretty doesn't count."

I wish Roger could have seen the *Ring* the New York Met put on a little later, with all the fairy tale scenery and costumes of the old legend. It was broadcast on four nights, and I videotaped it. I've played those tapes many times since. I would like to know what Roger— or Wagner!—might have said about that broadcast. The Sieglinde was a hefty black woman matched with an equally hefty white Siegmund as her brother lover. Not exactly the fairy tale twin look. But, oh, those voices. There is one part, when Sieglinde, pregnant by Siegmund, cries out to the Valkyries to save her child. Her voice rises into a full-throated passion that —even when I just think about it now—makes the hair on my neck rise and tears swell into my eyes.

I remember Roger sitting on his bed in his new—and last—home there in San Francisco, with the score beside him, conducting with a slim baton the prelude to *Tristan and Isolde* streaming from his CD player. Totally absorbed in the music. It was the last time I saw him.

Sometime after his death, a shipment of boxes arrived from his executor. It was Roger's vast and carefully selected collection of books about Wagner.

My father, John Sutcliffe, echoing a cheerful friend.

The Statue

WHEN a small Catholic church school in rural western Iowa gave up the Holy Ghost, all the stained glass windows and statuary ended up for sale at an antique shop frequented by Nance McMinimee, a friend and fellow member of the Southwest Iowa Tourism Committee.

I acquired first, through Nance, a large stained glass window with a round center panel featuring a painted pope or bishop's high hat. I would have preferred a lamb, but that was what was left at the antique dealer's, Nance said. The price was low and the window was colorful.

Not long after acquiring the window, during a visit to Nance and Howard's farm east of Denison, I admired the statue of St. Francis she had put in her backyard garden. "It's just plaster," she said, "but I gave it several coats of polyurethane, and it's holding up really well. I bought it at the same place I got your stained glass."

"Are there any statues left?" I asked.

"I think so," she answered. "Shall I pick up one for you?"

"Sure," I said. "I'd love to have a statue of David."

Obviously, I was not up to date on my Catholic saints' roster, as I don't think the statue of David in Florence, which was vaguely in my head, was ever considered among the saintly.

A few weeks later, Nance called to say she would pick me up by my pottery workshop in Audubon to go to Atlantic together for the next tourism meeting. "I'll stop by Lou's and see what statues he's got left," she said. "I'm driving the pickup."

"Try for David," I said.

Nance arrived in the farm pickup a couple hours later, with something in the truck bed rolled in quilts and held down with log chains. She was laughing so hard she could barely talk.

My father had been helping me mix clay in the pottery, and he came out the open overhead door to see what was going on. Nance finally caught her breath.

"Okay," she said, wiping her eyes. "There were only a few statues left at Lou's, and all were in bad shape except for this one. So we wrapped it up and loaded it on the truck.

"I drove off down Highway 141, but I stopped in Manning, along the highway, for a cup of coffee. As I came out of the coffee shop, I noticed an elderly couple walking away from my pickup, but I didn't think anything of it. People are always just nosey.

"I was going along 141 at a pretty brisk clip, as I was

now a little late. Then I see a red light behind me and it was blinking. Uh, oh, I'm thinking, he's caught me speeding, and that's not going to look good on my record.

"I pulled over, and the patrol car pulled up behind me. The guy gets out and comes toward me with his gun drawn."

My father blinked, and my eyebrows went skyward.

She continued, "'What have you got in the truck?' he says. And I start laughing, and I say, 'Louie put you up to this!' And he says, 'Lady, I'm not kidding you. You get out and show me what you've got back there.'

"So I get out of the cab and I go around back, and I pull the chain and the old quilt away from the front end of the statue, and he says, 'Jesus Christ!' and I say, 'You can say that again.'

"Then he starts to laugh. He says, 'This old couple found me in the coffee shop and told me there was a pickup outside with a dead body in it. Well, you know, you never know what weird things people do. I had to check it out. Sorry about that, ma'am,' he says, 'No problem. Get back on the road.'

"And I say, 'Officer, you missed your chance to catch me for speeding,' and he just grins and waves me on."

"Let's have a look at this," my dad said, and he unhooked the gate and carefully extracted Jesus from his winding sheet. I helped him carry the statue into the pottery. We stood it upright on the dusty concrete floor. It was about three-quarters life size. Jesus was very colorful in a pastel sort of way, but was possibly suffering from enlarged heart syndrome, as it was bulging on the front of his chest.

"His big toe is the only thing missing," said Nance, pulling it from her jeans pocket. "He was the only statue in decent condition."

Nance and I drove off to the tourism meeting, leaving my father in contemplation of the Lord.

I introduced Jesus the next morning to my part time employee, Millie Warren, the bright-eyed widow of a Hamlin junk dealer. Millie grew up in a Danish farm family and had a fine practical bent plus an appreciation of practical jokes, due to early life with several brothers.

After a few days had passed, Millie cornered me. "I can't take this," she said. "Every day when I walk in the door, I jump out of my skin, because I see him and I think it's some man in there."

Of a practical nature myself, I quickly figured out that the problem wasn't a religious but a gender one. So I got a yellow apron and a sunbonnet from my mother and decked out the newest employee. I put his toe in his apron pocket, figuring that was a good place to keep it until I got around to glueing it back on.

The transformation worked, and Millie was fine with her quiet coworker. But sometime after that, she reported confidentially to me that she'd heard some complaints around town. So Dad and I dragged the statue into the kiln room, which was always closed off, and the complaints ceased.

Jesus, still decked out in my mother's bonnet and apron, languished there for years, gathering dust, generally unnoticed. And then, in 1978, I moved to California. After it appeared that the move was permanent, my dad arranged to sell at auction my old Victorian house in Audubon, the furniture, and some of the things left in the pottery building, which my father owned.

After the auction, Dad called me in Santa Barbara, excited to tell me that I'd made about five thousand dollars, quite a bit more than either of us had expected. "Did you get rid of the Jesus statue?" I asked.

"Well," he said, "Not exactly. I had asked that new young auctioneer, Colonel Bruce, to handle the sale. When it was over and people were starting to leave the yard, I noticed the statue was still there by the barberry bushes, and he hadn't put it on the sale. So I said, 'Bruce, you forgot the Jesus statue.' And he said, 'Doc, I'm just starting in this auctioneering business, and if the word gets around that I sold Jesus, I'll never live it down.'"

"So what did you do with it," I asked, hoping he wasn't shipping it to Santa Barbara.

"Your friend, Nancy Carlson, Elmer's daughter, was there, and I just asked her if she'd get rid of it for me. She had her husband's pickup with her. I don't know what she did with it, but she took it."

A couple years passed, and then one day in early spring my phone in Santa Barbara rang, and it was Leroy Larsen.

He and Lorraine were farm friends of mine who were just retiring from their farm near Audubon. Leroy said, "We bought the last lot, maybe you know, on Circle Drive, and we're taking down Elmer Carlson's old farmhouse there, going to build our new ranch style house. But, Judy, that statue of Jesus you used to have is down in the basement. What do you want me to do with it?"

"Oh, Lord, Leroy, call my Dad!"

My father, retired from veterinary work, was quite active during those days with the local Historical Society. He had helped the organization acquire the old county home for the indigent, just south of town, and he and Mom and the other members, many on the elderly side, were attempting to turn the old two-story brick building into a local history museum. There was a pencil collection, a lot of old dresses and hats, some World War I and II uniforms, scrapbooks of newspaper clippings and postcards, several glass cases of stuffed birds, a room full of antique children's toys and clothing, and a room with a lectern, an old Bible, and a church pew.

On the phone, Dad said to me, "Some of the ladies have been putting together a Religion Room, and maybe I can put Jesus in there. They don't have too much collected just yet, and it'll perk things up."

The next week when I called home, I got my mother on the phone. "Did Dad get the statue upstairs into that Religion Room?"

My mother replied, "Well, not quite, honey. He and

Fred got it hauled as far as the basement of the museum. But then they found out that what they thought was a Religion Room was really a Lutheran Room. The ladies didn't want any Catholic statuary up there. Your dad and Fred had kind of had it at that point, and Fred said he'd just take it on home to the farm in his pickup and bury the darn thing. And that would be the end of it.

"But you know your dad. Fred had called him up later to tell him he'd buried the statue under the pine trees way back of the house. That was on Good Friday. Your dad was thinking he'd sneak out there early on Easter morning and dig it up.

"But thank goodness, there was a frost that morning, and he was all worried about his peach trees, and that kept him busy for a good while, and he forgot about it."

The Diver

Snickers in my sneakers. These leftover Halloween Snickers are pretty small, probably get smaller every year. But I like them, and they remind me of Paul Pettingill who often left nice, fat, full-size Snickers bars in my shoes.

I bought my house in Santa Barbara from Paul, thanks to a friendly real estate agent. She put me, young woman with little money, together with Paul, older guy wanting to sell his house, but not real sure about it. She told me that he was kind of shy and had said no to a couple potential buyers.

But she and I went over to his house on Cliff Drive. It was a small, stucco, flat-roofed house within a chain-link fenced yard, ivy on the fence. I liked it because there was a double garage next to the street, perfect for the tile painting studio I intended to set up.

A knock at the door introduced me to a very tall, lanky guy in his sixties, with curling hair of the pepper and salt variety. He tended to lower his head and not look directly when talking to me, just kind of sidewise.

There was a wagging black dog at his knees. We went into the small living room, and the real estate lady and Paul sat down on couch and chair. I went for the dog. I dropped onto the sculptured yellow carpeting and started petting the pooch at Paul's feet, giving my attention to the dog and letting the agent talk to Paul. I only said, "What's her name?"

"Blackie," said Paul.

The agent talked to Paul, I petted Blackie, and pretty soon I was signing some papers, and Paul was selling the house to me on contract for $77,000. That meant, I found out after we left, that I had to drum up $15,000 for a down payment within three months. I went back to my home in Iowa, worked hard, sold whatever I could to add to my savings account, and with a little help from my dad, made the payment.

Meanwhile, just before the closing, the agent called.

"Judy," she said, "I don't know if I mentioned that Paul is a deep sea diver. He was selling the house because he was going to be stationed in the Middle East. But that job just recently fell apart, so now he still needs a place to stay in Santa Barbara. He's wondering if you would rent him a room for awhile. I wouldn't worry, he's an okay guy."

"Uh, gee, sure. He seemed harmless." I said, shrugging my shoulders.

So, after the closing, I paid Paul, through the bank, $395 a month, and he paid me about $200 a month cash rent. I don't know if that was pure dumb luck or what, but for most of my first year in Santa Barbara it was Paul's rent money plus extremely frugal living on my part that kept me solvent while I started up a tile mural painting business from scratch.

At the time I joined the household, Paul had already moved his furniture and, apparently, the dog out of the house to some place in Hawaii where he had an apartment. He'd left a glass-topped small dining table in the little dining nook. I picked up some cheap chairs at a garage sale. And that was it for furniture for both of us. I slept on the floor in my sleeping bag in the master bedroom, the one connected directly to a bathroom. Paul slept on his sleeping bag in one of the other two bedrooms and used the other bath in the hallway. This was high living to me, after the old Victorian house I'd had in Iowa, with a shower that froze in the wintertime.

Paul left his outdoor shoes on the carpet near the front door entrance, Japanese style. So I did the same.

After the first couple slightly nervous nights with a strange man in the house, I quickly got used to his quiet presence. He would leave early in the morning to go to work, and come home late. Sometimes we'd share beans and rice for supper, and then he'd talk a bit about his work. He had very large hands, and he'd tip his tall head and hunch his shoulders a little and say that deep sea diving wasn't much.

"I'm just a welder," he'd say. "I just happen to weld under water."

He told me about how slowly a diver has to return to

the ocean surface, how deadly it can be if the diver rushes the ascent for any reason. Once at the surface, the diver has to rest in some kind of pressure tank for maybe another hour until his body has recovered.

"You just have to be patient," he said. "Over the years I've seen several of my buddies die from moving up too fast. The last one, just a few months ago, was a guy I'd worked with for years and years.

"And you never know whether he did it on purpose," he added, looking at his blunt fingernails, "or just got impatient."

I thought maybe he dived in the sleek wetsuits worn by all the slim teenage boys cavorting in the surf down on the beach. A wide grin broke across his face.

"I'll show you one of these days," he said.

Several days later he returned early one evening and called me to come out to the driveway by the garage where his car was parked. He pulled a huge yellow mass of rubbery material out of the car. "Here, put this on," he said, and held up his diving suit for me to try to climb into. It was way too long for me, but I scrunched up the leggings so I could stand up in it. It was extremely heavy and awkward. I could hardly move.

Then Paul fetched the head mount from the car. It looked just like the old drawings I'd seen of divers' helmets, a big round metal casing with an oval glass window with bars on the front and something like lug nuts around the shoulders to attach it.

I managed to stand still under all that weight and not breathe much until he'd shambled back to the car and returned with a little camera to capture what would have made a terrific Halloween costume, had I been able to breathe and walk.

Paul was very near retirement and intended to enjoy it in Hawaii, so he was very attuned to correct diving procedures. There was a Japanese waitress in Hawaii he had been friends with over the years, and maybe she would be part of his future.

As my first year in Santa Barbara rounded to a close and Paul's move to Hawaii loomed near, my commissions for bath and kitchen murals were picking up nicely. I even bought a papaya. And every now and then I found Snickers bars in my shoes by the door.

There was an old but heartily producing avocado tree in the backyard that Paul and I both enjoyed immensely. And I was intrigued with a small apple tree squeezed into the few feet of sideyard between the back of the house and the neighbor's fence. It actually bore excellent apples and sometimes had apple blossoms on its branches at the same time as ripe apples. It must have been developed especially for Southern California climate. One day I noticed a weather-worn tag tied to a lower branch. It stated the sun and rain requirements of the tree and showed its varietal name as a Pettingill Apple. I asked Paul how come the tree had his name.

He had no idea.

On the Street

UNUSUAL PEOPLE walk or roll the streets of Santa Barbara. Not too different from other cities, I suppose, but there probably aren't many places where in December I would have seen a slim guy in a Santa hat, coat, beard, and slim red tights sailing forth on roller skates from a bank parking lot.

I sometimes wonder if he was the same guy who was nearly naked—his lean loins girded with ivy—and painted green from his curly head of hair to his inline skates. He floated nonchalantly down State Street as part of the Summer Solstice parade, turning in easy circles, round and round.

A memorable walker in that same parade was an extremely pregnant woman in a belly dance costume, belly totally exposed, with a large, purple eye painted over the blossoming navel.

Those were the flamboyant ones. There were others, not quite so startling, but the eyes they'd catch would linger, and the heads would turn.

One of my favorites was a young woman, stunningly

beautiful, very slim, with a long, exquisite neck, reminding me always of Masai warriors, and a thin, slightly aquiline nose, dusky lidded dark eyes, and very short tightly curled black hair. Every once in a while I'd see her walking dreamily along State Street, usually alone. I'd watch the people she passed turn around to stare after her.

One day I caught sight of her near the Lobero Theater downtown. She was crossing the street with several children following after her. She was dancing her way across the avenue, the children loping and hopping after her, like a scene from the Pied Piper of Hamelin. Sometimes I wanted to find out who she was, but mostly I just enjoyed the occasional mystery of her magical presence on Santa Barbara streets.

There was one other street walker I frequently wondered about. I would spot him walking along Cliff Drive as I was driving my VW downtown. A well-built black man in a pinstriped, three-piece banker's suit, with a white handkerchief in the pocket, and wearing a black fedora. He strolled along the sidewalk, almost always alone, with a sauntering gait, a tall proud posture, and a smile on his face. I always figured he must be whistling a happy tune as I whizzed by. I almost missed seeing his white cane.

Every Friday morning I had breakfast with Rita Shaw at the Mesa Cafe, halfway between my house and her apartment. We always had a good time talking about everything and anything. When the Mesa Cafe underwent remodeling, we shifted our Friday location to a small diner half a block away, with booths and a counter.

And guess who walked in and sat at that counter. The well-dressed gentleman with the white cane. Rita and I sat in our booth and watched him, silently. He ordered "the usual," and a plate of eggs and toast appeared. We watched him extend his fingers lightly to locate the salt and pepper the waitress had placed in front of him, and he dusted his eggs. He very neatly downed them, and then took out his wallet, stroked a bill between his fingers, then handed it to the waitress, who gave him some change. After a little final banter with the waitress, he turned on the bar stool, took his cane, and nonchalantly walked out the door.

The next Friday at the diner, he again came in and sat down at the counter. I hopped up and stood next to him. "I'm Judy, and my friend Rita and I are sitting in the booth behind you. Would you care to join us?"

"I'm James," he said, with a nice smile. He took my arm and sat down on one side of the booth, Rita and I on the other.

He was pleasant and talkative, and very open. So I asked what had happened to him.

"Well, I retired from the post office," he said. "And I'd split with my wife by then, so I was living alone in an apartment downtown. I was enjoying life, and I liked going dancing. One Saturday night I was getting dolled up to go dancing, when the lights went out. Dang, I thought, I was only half shaven. Then the lights went back on, so I finished the shave. Then they went out again. And then I wondered if the electricity was off, how come the radio was still playing.

"Well, I thought, I must be blind.

"So I didn't go to the dance, and I sat around that night and worried myself to death, but by morning, I was kinda used to it. So I found my way downstairs and was groping my way down the street because I was out of milk, needed some groceries. A buddy of mine saw me and said, 'What's the matter with you, James, you blind or something?'

"Yeah, I said, I think I am.

"'Well, stay right here, and I'll go get you a cane,' he said. And he did. So I got around okay. Then I took a class on how to read braille, but I wasn't too good at that. I learned to read a braille watch, though," he said, and extended his wrist far enough from his white shirt cuff to expose his watch.

"How do you know what kind of dollar bills you've got?" I asked.

"Oh, that's easy," he said, "they feel different. I just have to feel them and I can tell."

"Do you ever get depressed?" Rita asked.

"Oh, no," he said. "Just the first few days. I got used to it quick. I'm as happy as can be now, just the way things are. I wouldn't change it now if I could."

When we got up to leave, Rita and I each gave James a

hug. James held on to me a long time. "Umm, Judy, you do give the best hugs. When are you here for breakfast again, girl?" I looked at Rita with a raised eyebrow. She shrugged and grinned, and I said, "Well, here or at the Mesa Cafe, most every Friday."

We had quite a few hugs from James over the next few weeks and months. If Rita and I wanted to talk about other things, we'd just go down to the Pelican Beach restaurant by the ocean instead.

A couple times I saw James walking around downtown. He was perfectly capable of getting across city streets, stop lights and all, by himself, but I'd observe him happily accepting the arm of a lady to assist him in crossing. I think he did quite well in finding female companionship. He was very dapper and very warm.

He had asked me my phone number when we first met, and he called me up many times. He'd just chat a little bit was all. Just wanted to check that he remembered the number. Wondering if we were going to breakfast on Friday. "I sure do need one of those hugs!" he'd say.

And one time he called and said he was planning on going to some big whing ding in Canada. Olympics, maybe. Some big affair that I don't remember. And he wondered if I'd like to go with him for a couple weeks. He'd pay my way if I'd accompany him.

I didn't take him up on the offer. But sometimes I think I missed an opportunity.

Unions

J
EXITED COLLEGE with an extreme liberal bias against business and businessmen. But I had to make my way in that
world. I had no plan. It had never occurred to me while at
the University of Iowa studying what I loved, English and
Chinese, that I should be thinking about what I was going
to do after I graduated.

When that moment arrived with my cap and gown, I
decided on impulse to follow the example of a small town
woman in a book I'd read, *Sister Carrie*, by Theodore Dreiser.
She went to work in Chicago. So I went to work in Chicago,
a big city where I'd never been. A girlfriend from college said
she'd go with me, a partner in new adventures.

My father, who was rarely ill, took to his bed the summer day Evie and I left by bus to connect with the train to
Chicago. I was too excited about seeing a big city to ponder
why my father had collapsed that day. A stoic and silent man,
he couldn't express what he felt.

Soon Evie and I had a little second floor brownstone

apartment. It was furnished with a few basic pieces of furniture but no silverware or dishes. We bought plates and cups at Goodwill and ate lunches a few times at a Chinese restaurant, taking the chopsticks home. We worked on our chopstick expertise until we could even pick up Jello.

An employment agency found me a job. They didn't seem to care about my degree, just wanted to know what practical work experience I'd had. I'd worked summers for the local Audubon, Iowa, weekly paper. So they sent me off on journalism job possibilities, and I took the first one offered, as a receptionist and potential writer/editor at a small ad agency that specialized in writing and printing employee newsletters for good-sized industrial corporations around the city.

This was in 1963. Offices merely had typewriters and mimeographs. Our professional looking newsletters were set in letterpress type. My fingers were smudged with ink any time I did proofreading or attempted to cut and paste with scissors and rubber cement, before sending the galleys back to the printer.

After a few months, I was promoted to assisting the three editors. For the first time I got to see the inside of an actual factory, one of the locations of Hammond Organ Company. The building seemed enormous. I tailed after our tall blonde woman editor as we walked briskly with the corporate personnel manager through several departments and down into a windowless basement area. Rows of big steel punch presses made a horrendous racket, slamming and banging. I was horrified to see that almost all the presses were operated by black men handcuffed to the machines. Someone explained to me that these were old and outdated punch presses, made without safety features. The wrist cuffs assured that the man's hands could not be under the whacking mechanism when it pounded down with fierce and ponderous weight. We wrote a story about this particular punch press department, giving credit to the men for hard work, and being exceedingly careful to spell every man's name correctly.

Actually, what we wrote was capitalist propaganda. We sold these newsletters to companies that either didn't have a union and didn't want one, or did have a union and wanted to keep peace. We wrote articles that explained why earning a profit was necessary to a business, why the company was like a happy family, why everyone enjoyed their work. Maybe the punch presses pounded my head, but after a while I began to believe the stuff we—and I—were writing.

Part of it was encountering Ayn Rand's book, *Atlas Shrugged,* one of the few pro-capitalism, pro-industry novels ever written, and a very compelling one. Part of it was asking punch press machine workers why they liked their job, and getting over and over again the surprising statement, "the variety of the work."

And part of it was interviewing the executives and managers of whatever departments we would be featuring in upcoming issues. After awhile I got rather canny about guessing which managers had read *Atlas Shrugged.* The Hammond

Organ director of manufacturing told me he had not only read it, he'd given a copy to each of his managers. "One of them," he said, "came into my office and said, 'Now I understand you.'"

Within my first year of work, I was given the newsletter responsibility for a new client, Rivington Electric Company. They had plants in Chicago, Milwaukee, and Los Angeles.

Wearing what women wore in those days, a dress or suit, nylons, high heels, coat, hat, and gloves, I took buses to the Chicago plant to meet initially with the Vice President of Personnel. I was 23.

MacDonald's office was small and uncluttered. No hint of what the man might be interested in. I sat primly on a metal chair near his desk, waiting for him to show up.

A stocky, broad-chested man, nearly bald, strode into the room, and the atmosphere swirled around him like a storm in the desert sands. Though he stopped still, there was boundless energy about him. His face was scarred, scars across his cheek. His nose had probably been broken.

He sat down and we quickly went over my suggestions for the first issue of his newsletter. "We have a rather strong and active union," he said, "but I can always talk to them. I want my men to feel that they are important. That the work they do well is appreciated." We quickly agreed on several articles to start off with. He would connect me with various supervisors so I could interview employees and write the stories. "Stop and talk to me again before you leave, and then let me know when you'll be back with the rough draft," he said, and he introduced me to his assistant before he left.

Having lived in a small town with a weekly newspaper, I understood quite well what it means to people to occasionally get their name and their photo in the newspaper for raising the county's largest zucchini or becoming an Eagle Scout. It makes people feel worthwhile.

Mac was 42, married, with a teenage son. The more often I went to the plant, the more my anticipation at being with Mac for a few minutes grew. His presence was invigorating. Our consultations about the newsletter began to take longer and longer. Other topics than newsletters crept in around the edges of conversation. And one late afternoon, he offered to drive me back to my Old Town apartment and suggested we might have dinner together first.

I am always calm, and so I wasn't quite certain why he seemed upset, stubbing out several cigarettes in a row, during dinner in a small restaurant downtown. I took the opportunity of silence on his part to ask about the scars on his face.

"I was a teenager, running with a bunch of other boys, drinking too much," he said. "We all piled into a car, six of us, and drove too fast. We were drunk and crazy. We crashed the car and every kid but me was killed. I was pallbearer for every one of my friends. I should have died with them. Every minute since then I have taken as a gift, and I work and I play as hard as I can with those moments left to me."

He parked his car in front of my apartment house, the radio playing softly. I fumbled for the door handle. "Don't go yet. Stay a while," he said. "I don't know how to say this, but I want you." I turned to stare wide-eyed at him. He gripped the steering wheel, looking straight ahead into the dark street.

"I'm fighting it because I'm married, I love my wife and my son, and I've never done this before. The song that's playing now, *Walk Away*, is how I feel. I need to just walk away from you, but right now I can't." He turned to me. "I want to see your apartment."

I wasn't sure what was happening, but Evie was on vacation, the apartment was empty. We walked up the stairs and into the two rooms. He strode into the middle of the living room-bedroom space, his entry forceful and direct. He was not a man to dawdle at the edges. He threw his hat on the bed, and encircled me in his arms, kissing me until I was breathless and dizzy. We fell upon the bedcovers, embracing, fully clothed.

"If I were inside you," he said, "you'd be pregnant right now."

Lucky for me, the sexual revolution was in full swing, and birth control pills were available by prescription, if one could get up courage enough to approach a possibly sternly disapproving physician. It was very easy, actually. The doctor listened to me talk around Robin Hood's barn for a few minutes, and then smiled gently and said, "Why don't you just use birth control pills? Here, I'll write out a prescription for you."

Thus began my first affair. And ended my sharing an apartment with Evie. She was appalled at my behavior, and hurt, and she moved back to Iowa City. I took a new, modern apartment that I could just barely afford, a couple blocks down the street, and began my life alone.

Intimacy brings forth insight. Mac cared deeply for the men employed at the plant, and he liked to talk about them with me. I went to the company Christmas party and watched how he dipped up punch for the men. He had arranged the glass cups on the table in front of him, and he'd motion to each man to pick one up, while he greeted him, joked with him. Then, as he carefully poured the spiked pink liquid, he had the opportunity to steady each man's hand on the little cup with his, making that slight physical connection with each one. There are many things that make good managers. And some are as small as a touch.

He knew his men very well. Almost too well. He was very jovial one night. Laughing, he told me that they'd had a really rough month financially at the plant. The president of the company had met with him to explain that a temporary shortfall in cash meant that they couldn't make payroll. He didn't want to go to the bank for it. "Do you suppose there's any way you could get the men to go out on strike for a few days?" he asked Mac.

"How long you want them out?" Mac answered. He

knew the men and the workings of the union bosses so well, that he managed to say just the right thing to make them mad enough to strike the plant for about a week. Then he patched things up, and they all came back to work, and all got paid.

Ayn Rand, I thought, would have liked this man. So, too, Cleopatra. Her evocations of Marc Antony described Mac to me. "His delights were dolphin-like, they showed his back above the element they lived in."

Our meetings, over the next two or three years, until I left Chicago for Germany, were few but intense. The last time we were together in the city, it was raining, and the dark streets were streaked in neon. Approaching a stoplight, we watched the changing columns of green, yellow, and red light in the glistening street ahead. "My life is full," he said.

I only saw him once more, in Santa Barbara, over a decade later. He'd come out West to visit their Los Angeles plant, and he detoured to Santa Barbara to spend a night with me. We were a little awkward with each other. He seemed smaller and thinner. He was happy to see me in my own entrepreneurial business. I took a photo of him, of his face, the only one I have, and the scars show in the flattening light of the flash.

I didn't hear from him again, and I would never have called the plant to ask for him. But I sent him an innocuous Christmas card at the plant address. A note came back from the man who had been his assistant in earlier days, saying that he was sorry to tell me that Mac had died. I knew only a small part of his life and nothing about his death, except that he loved every moment he had been given.

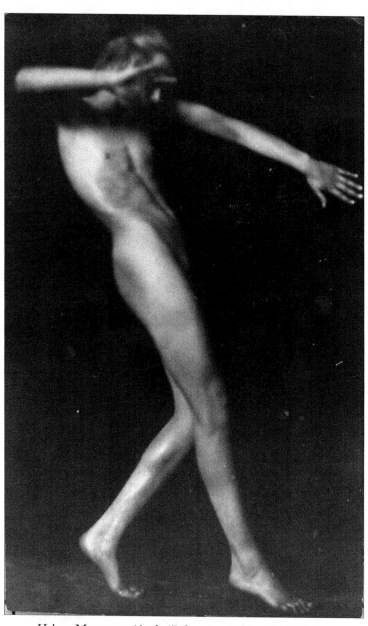

*Helena Mayer, age 12. At 17 she won a gold medal in fencing
at the 1928 Olympics in Amsterdam.*

The Olympian

W HAT SHOULD I DO with these photographs? Norbert Schiller gave them to me before he died in 1988. Nude photos of Helene Mayer when she was very young. He gave me his small parchment briefcase as well, and I've kept them there all these years. Never shown them to anyone. Yet something so beautiful should be seen. She looked like a statue of a Greek goddess come to life.

Helene Mayer was an Olympic champion fencer, ranked by *Sports Illustrated* as one of the 100 greatest female athletes of the twentieth century. Tucked in a tiny leather folder in Norbert's case is a 1968 German stamp with her famous profile. She wore her long blonde braids in nautilus rings on either side of her head, tightly bound with a white band.

She and Norbert were lovers when she was very young and he a decade older. She was born in 1910.

Norbert was born in Vienna in 1899. I think they met when he was part of the ensemble of actors at the theater in Frankfurt and she was in the upper classes at a girls school, high school age. He was a romantic heartthrob on the stage in those years and had many young, enamored fans. She was already winning major fencing matches.

In the suitcase with the photos is a short story he wrote. It was printed in a newspaper, probably in Berlin in the late 1920s or early '30s, when short stories and plays by Norbert often appeared, before Hitler wrecked the world. It's in old-style German type, hard for me to decipher. But I can read quite a bit of it. It describes a young girl standing by her bicycle under a blossoming chestnut tree, "her head with its blonde braids lifted and attentive, like a deer just before it steps from the forest to the meadow." She is watching the rear doors of the theater as the actors arrive to ready for the evening performance. She appears to be waiting, looking for someone. The young hero walks by, and "even in his civilian clothing, a sword seems to swing and thunder crash." The young girl blushes, her cheeks "rosy like semi-transparent Chinese porcelain. . . . Only someone sixteen knows these swelling sighs, the interrupted breathing, the reddening cheeks."

In the suitcase are two unusual photos of Helene Mayer very young. They appear to be solemn modern dance poses. She is nude and, though tall and thin, there is no roundness yet developed. She is all straightness and flatness, bent in dynamic angles, as though posing for an Art Deco bas relief.

But when the body bloomed, it took away everyone's breath. There were little statues of Helene Mayer in homes everywhere in Germany in her Olympic years, in her fencing tunic and her coiled braids.

Norbert gave me a handful of snapshots in black and white, taken, I think he said, on the beach of Gerhart Hauptmann's island. There are photos of a statuesque, nude Helene standing on a large rock, one arm stretched out to sea, the other raised to the sky. In another she is stretched out on the same boulder, looking up at her little naked brother. With one leg extended at length, she looks like a mermaid gliding toward the boy. In another, the boy is standing just beyond Norbert, both nude, and the youth is pointing out to sea. Whenever I read Thomas Mann's *Death in Venice*, I think of this photograph of the blond boy looking out to sea.

In another photo, taken closer in, a lean, naked Norbert with thick black hair curling down over his eyebrows sits in the sand facing a goddess who appears to be made of bronze. One leg is flat in the sand, the other raised. The latter is a perfect long-thighed leg, with white sand crusting the lower perimeter. Her breasts are perfect, statuesque, with the fullness of persimmon fruit. Her hair is very light, pulled neatly into a braided bun at the nape of her neck. Her head leans shyly and serenely downward. Someone, I assume Norbert, in an attempt at a shadowed modesty, has scribbled with a pen across his revealed pubic area.

There is another photo taken at a different place, but a similar time, heads in close up. Her face is on the left, looking right, in profile, her hair in braided loops below her ears.

Norbert, with his dark hair brushed back, looks at her from under his long, dark eyelashes. On the photo he or she wrote: Die Frage an das Schicksal. The question of destiny, or our destiny or fate.

He had asked her to marry him, and her mother was for it. But "The Golden He" (her nickname, pronounced Hay) refused. She was very young and there was too much career directly in front of her. She lived and breathed the sport of fencing.

In 1928 she won the gold medal in the Amsterdam Olympics. Plus national and international contests. By 1932, however, she was in Claremont, California, studying at Scripps College. Her Jewish heritage was responsible for the leap away from Germany. From there she went to Mills College in Northern California, where she began teaching both sports and languages. In 1936, warned by the Nazis that her parents in Germany would be punished if she did not return, she took part in the Berlin Olympics, taking the Silver Medal in fencing. She returned to Mills College and became an American citizen, but after the war, in 1952, homesick, she returned to Germany, married a wealthy baron, and died of breast cancer in 1953, not quite 42 years old.

Also in the case is a letter from Helene to Norbert in those final years, and another letter from her mother to Norbert, telling him that she is in great physical distress, unable any longer to write, waiting to die.

What should I do with these photographs? And with

the several short stories Norbert wrote about Helene Mayer? His wife, Mary, is now 82 and becoming forgetful. She told me several times on the phone recently, "I miss Norbert so much. He had good taste in women. I've never been jealous in my life. I don't know what it's like."

His son, Norbert, Jr., a very fine freelance photographer of the Middle East's wars and wines, is moving his family out of Lebanon and Oman to the snowy winters of Minnesota. Not a stable situation, perhaps.

Norbert's daughter Daniela is divorced with two teenage boys. Her house in Montecito was totally destroyed in the 2008 fire. She lost everything. Nothing left of her father's mementoes that she treasured. Maybe I'll send it all to her someday. If she promises to keep it in a bank vault, not a California house.

But none of them read German. I am perplexed by the remains of love affairs of the dead.

Die Frage an das Schicksal

The Wave

JT WAS SUMMER, the corn was high and green, and I was driving my little old red VW bug into Des Moines to buy some ceramic glazes I needed for my pottery business.

It was a glorious day to drive, one of those days when Iowa is greener than Ireland could possibly be and full of good cheer because there's been enough rain and enough sun, and the farmers know their crop is going to be a good one. Green corn and green money in the bank.

I was moving right along on Interstate 80. That little bug could fly. I was singing to myself and the corn gods. I had to concentrate on driving. I zipped around a silvery car. No idea what kind it was, the only cars I recognize are bugs and 1958 Fords. I barely noticed the man behind the wheel.

The silver car followed behind me for awhile, and then gracefully pulled forward in the passing lane and went around me. I could see the back of the guy's head, his grey hair, but that was all. No one else in his car.

He lost a little speed going up the next hill, so I pulled into the left lane and sailed past him again.

Another mile or two, and he speeded up and pulled even with my little VW, didn't look my way, but just held the same pace for a few moments, and then pulled ahead and was once again ahead of me.

Now I realized there was a little car game going on here. So I just buzzed right around him again, but never looked at him while passing. Though I tried to see what he looked like in the rear view mirror and failed.

We played this intertwining game of passing cars for more than 40 miles.

I could see ahead of us the first exits to West Des Moines. As I approached the Valley West exit, I plunked on my turning signal, just as the silver car started to pass me one more time.

As I headed downward onto the ramp, I looked up at the highway just in time to see the silver car pass by. Sunlight sparkled on its chrome. An arm was extended high above the roof of the car in a farewell salute.

The Connection

Mr. Joseph might have lived forever if they hadn't taken away his telephone.

He and his brother left Germany when the Nazis took power. He helped set up the film division for Brooks Institute of Photography in Santa Barbara. After the war he was invited by the city of Munich to found an international film museum there, which he did. He finally was united with the actress who had been the long love of his life. He remained in Germany until she died. And then, in his 80s, not in the best of health, he moved back to Santa Barbara, because he had always felt safe and happy there. His brother, a film editor, lived in Los Angeles and was also on his last legs. He died first.

Rudolf Joseph was a tall, stately, white-haired man, with an eagle's nose and eyes that probed to the core. He must have been very imposing in his younger years, before his legs began to give out. He had been assistant producer to several famous stage and screen directors as a young man in the theatrically vibrant between-war years in Germany.

179

He was exceptional at casting and scheduling. Those skills came in handy in his fading years, after his Santa Barbara physician told him he was depressed and needed "stimulation." He solved this by putting a want ad on a nearby college bulletin board for students to cook evening dinners for him. He cast only young, pretty girls in this companionate role, their cooking talents being of lesser stimulant interest than youth and gender. He loved listening to their patter and took on the role himself of a kindly grandfather who listened and occasionally advised, based on long and worldly experience.

I met him during this part of his life, intrigued by his German theater experience and his love of music. He enjoyed my company as well, because I loved the German language, opera—especially *Der Rosenkavalier*— and lieder. I spent every Wednesday evening with him for several years, consuming in the process a great deal of poached salmon and Asti Spumante. "Please, may I pour you another glass?" he would say, and, because it was sweetly addictive, I would happily nod.

He was writing his memoirs of the theater world of Berlin between the wars when I first knew him. The book was published in Germany. A film crew from Germany came once to interview and film him in a documentary they were making about the famous German director Pabst.

In those years, he was able to go up and down the stairs to his apartment over a garage. And we would go to international films together with gusto. But his legs gradually weakened. He had had polio as a boy. And he was gaining weight, a considerable thickening around the middle. He was not fond of exercise, and he was fond of eating.

Eventually, he began hiring, along with the chorus of girls, a young male student who could help him around the apartment. He no longer went downstairs at all. He acquired one of those gadgets older people wear around their necks that phone for help in case of a fall. He used it a few times. Normally, it brought his helpful landlady from next door. But as he grew heavier, a heftier rescue crew would arrive.

His landlady worried about him, as did various of his friends. A home health aid woman was hired to come every day and check on him. His condition was not improving. Yet he was always cheerful, always interested in the life of the world, and he continued to schedule the frisky maidens to come and talk to him about their boyfriends and uncertain careers.

He lived with a portable telephone in his hand, and this was before the advent of ubiquitous cell phones. He was connected.

He also was unafraid of death. It was something we agreed upon. I had run across a very unusual book, ostensibly pulled from the stratosphere by a particularly interesting medium, Jane Roberts. It was called *The Afterdeath Journal of an American Philosopher: William James.* There was one chapter especially appealing to both of us. I made him a copy of that chapter, and once or twice during the years we visited, he would ask me for another copy.

The chapter began with these words: "Nowhere have I encountered the furnishings of a conventional heaven, or glimpsed the face of God. On the other hand, certainly I dwell in a psychological heaven by earth's standards, for everywhere I sense a presence, or atmosphere, or atmospheric presence that is well-intentioned, gentle yet powerful, and all-knowing. This seems to be a psychological presence of such stunning parts, however, that I can point to no one place and identify it as being there in contrast to being someplace else. At the risk of understating, this presence seems more like a loving condition that permeates existence, and from which all existence springs."

When he could no longer get out of bed by himself, his landlady declared that something else had to happen, and by whatever means he got there, the next time I went to visit him, he was in a small room in a private care center that had a huge, colorful garden just outside his doorway. He was able to sit up in bed and watch the birds in the garden, but that was about it. He remained cheerful, though communication with a Spanish-speaking maid was complex, and he was always pleased when I phoned to see if he was "at home" for a visit.

His income derived from the sale over time of his collection of Renaissance drawings that his acute eye had been collecting since he dropped out of high school in Frankfurt in order to work in an art gallery, art being his major interest along with theater and film. The drawings were held somewhere in London, and he would phone and talk to the gallery about which ones to put up for sale.

The years extended, but the drawings gave out, and there was no more money. "I have lived too long," he said to me, his false teeth sliding about a little, a wry look in his eyes.

The next time I visited him, urged by his ex-landlady, who kept track of him, he was in a county nursing home, in a double room, with some addled, prattling man in the next bed. Mr. Joseph rolled his eyes at that, but chatted happily with me about a current French film I'd seen.

And then, probably due to lack of funds, they took away his telephone. The landlady told me that when they did that, he stopped eating. And died.

She didn't know what to do with a lot of books that were left in his apartment, so she loaded up my Volkswagen with stacks of gallery auction books of Renaissance drawings, several plays in Italian (Greek to me), and a few poetry books in German.

What she couldn't find, and the one thing I would have especially treasured, was a tiny stuffed toy, a rabbit, that he had kept with him since he was a boy. It was always by his bedside.

My parents, John and Marjorie Sutcliffe, in their
cabin in the woods in mid 1950s. My mother
was born in 1908, my father in 1916.

The Radio

ONE LAST STROKE in her mid-eighties knocked out my mother's short term memory and left her long term memory in patches. Her sweet and social self remained. She would introduce visitors to the Alzheimers Wing to the residents, making up names for everyone as she went along. She was still trying to make the human connections she had always been good at in earlier days. Most of the time she remembered my name, and she never forgot my father.

She had always been Dad's partner in his veterinary business in Audubon, Iowa. She took care of the office at one end of our house, chatting with the farmers, always looking for creative potential to encourage. "You play any instrument?" she'd inquire of a new farmer. "We've got a little band at the Historical Society called the Country Heirs. If you play anything, come and make music with them."

Mom mixed up hog medicine, typed up labels, answered the phone, did the books, and took care of the foundlings a veterinarian household occasionally inherited. We had a baby screech owl for one summer. It perched on top the high shelving Dad had built for medicine storage, facing the outer office where farmers in their muddy boots would lean on the pass-through counter and chat with my mother. They'd talk and talk, and the owl would sit on top the shelves unmoving, like a stuffed toy. And then suddenly it would blink, and the farmer's mouth would drop open, or, worse, the owl would toddle over to the edge of the shelving and drop a wad of poop off the precipice. "Oh, haven't you met our little owl?" Mom would say to the pop-eyed farmer. "His name's WOL, like in Winnie the Pooh. Did you ever read that book to your children?" And she'd patiently mop up the floor.

Dad had the first short wave radio in the county, back in the late 1940s. He had a portable unit, an olive-colored metal box, about the size of a bread box, in his Jeep, and Mom had the base unit in the laundry room in a shoulder-high, green-stained wooden case that Dad had made for it. This was mighty high tech for those days. Dad could be working at a farm north of town, and Mom could call him and save time and gas on the next call. "KAC939 Base calling Car Number One," she'd intone into the hand-held microphone. "Could you stop at Dale Henriksen's on your way back into town? He thinks there's something wrong with that pregnant mare. Oh, and ask Ruth if she's going to bring sandwiches or cookies to the next Historical Society meeting, would you?"

I was still living in Santa Barbara at the time my mother

had that last stroke. Dad had been able to take care of her at home up to that time, but now it was necessary to move her to the Friendship Home. It was just three blocks away, and he'd walk up there once or twice every day to visit her and bring her flowers or an apple off the tree in his backyard. He spent the rest of his time making woodcarving caricatures of local folks and their farm animals, dogs, and cats. The John Sutcliffe Veterinarian sign that had hung near the office door for many years now read John Sutcliffe Woodcarver, and many of the same farmers who used to come for calf medicine would stop in to ask him to carve Uncle Harvey with a really big fish or Aunt Donna with a rolling pin in hand.

That was the state of things in January of 1996 when I sold my house in Santa Barbara and moved back to Audubon, into a charming, little 1920s bungalow I'd bought for a pittance.

After the initial depressing introduction to the Alzheimers group, I began to rather enjoy the visits. Minds may have been messed up, but frequently there were still personalities visible. One dear old woman every afternoon very carefully folded up all her clothes, packed them neatly into a suitcase, and sat down to wait for her son to come and get her. Around supper time one of the nurses or aides would go tell her that her son had phoned and wasn't able to come today. She would then carefully unpack everything and put her clothes away in the closet and drawers. To wait and repeat it all again the next day.

And there was the feisty little farm woman who'd be sitting quietly at a table, staring at nothing, and suddenly she'd yell in a loud and matriarchal voice, "Don't let that chicken get away!"

Dad saw the humor, and chuckled over it with me, but underneath, he desperately missed my mother's presence in his home and his bed. They had been so close over many years, both of them survivors of the Dust Bowl in Kansas and the Depression.

Not long after I returned to the Midwest, Dad told me that he'd developed some kind of blood disease, and it was slowly sapping his energy and strength. By the end of March he started getting a weekly blood transfusion, which made him feel a lot perkier.

In April a letter came from the state sesquicentennial committee saying that he'd been chosen as one of a hundred Iowa craftsmen who'd represent the state for two weeks that summer on the mall in Washington, DC. He was to take his woodcarvings of local people and farm animals to show, and he was to teach soap carving to children.

We sat at his kitchen table and thought about what to do. I filled out the acceptance form for him until I got to the line that asked if the person had any medical problems. Dad and I looked each other in the eye. For him, this was a chance of a lifetime. "What the heck," I said, and I wrote "No" on the line.

The week before we left for Washington that July, Dad

plumped himself up with several transfusions. He was so happy to be part of this big state celebration and to show the woodcarvings he'd made since he'd retired. He talked and joked with crowds of appreciative people who walked by the booths in the woodcarving section. He chatted with the two other woodcarvers and with a woman who was a cowboy poet. He showed gaggles of little kids how to carve rabbits and dogs out of bars of Ivory soap. I tagged around, watched, and assisted.

He made it through the first week okay, but by the weekend he knew he was wearing thin and told me he had to get another transfusion. So we took a cab to Georgetown Hospital. We sat in the ER lobby for eight hours before any doctor was free of incoming shootings and stabbings and could look at my waning dad. "I just need a transfusion, and I'll be out of here," he said to the doctors, but they insisted on putting him to bed and running an angioplasty. There wasn't much we could do until they'd gone through their list of required tests.

So for a couple days while he remained in the hospital, I sat at his booth and showed off his carvings. And I took a deep breath and taught flocks of little kids how to carve soap with plastic knives.

"You're getting pretty good at that," Dad grinned when he returned with enough new red blood cells to get him through the week. He went right back to his booth and had a very good time talking about woodcarving and Midwest farming with the city folk who stopped by. But he let me continue teaching soap carving to rambunctious kids.

He made it through the fall, and, in fact, started on a big new project to fence in an area of the old county home property and start an elk herd. He carved and painted an elk family from basswood and on Saturdays he'd sit down at the supermarket with that carving and sell lottery tickets for it, proceeds to go to the elk project. A tall, heavy-duty fence gradually wrapped around a pasture area set aside by the county for the potential elk.

It was around the end of January 1997, when Dad was approaching his eightieth birthday, when the transfusions began to lose their ability to charge him up. He wrote a letter to my sister Juanita in Kansas City and to me telling us that he wanted no resuscitation and no funeral services. Just cremation, his ashes to wait for my mother's and then to be scattered under pines in a woodland he loved. He was too tired now to make the daily trip to the Friendship Home to visit Mom. So I did the daily visits.

Even though I was her only visitor now, Mom would often smile when I came to her room, and she'd say, pointing to some plastic flowers on her dresser, "Daddy came this morning and brought me flowers. Aren't they pretty?"

"They're really nice, Mom," I'd say. "He's always so thoughtful, isn't he?"

Finally the transfusions proved useless, and in early February Dad ended up in the local hospital. Several of the men who'd worked with him on the elk project came to his room with a video to show him the young male and female elk they had just purchased to start the herd. They were to be delivered in the spring.

Towards the end of that week and a half, I slept fitfully on the floor near his bed at night. In the last two days, he descended into a coma. The young librarian Dad had helped raise money for a new library came to say goodby, as did a young man who used to go arrowhead hunting with him. The three of us sat around his bed and talked about the good times we had had. Suddenly my father groaned and straightened up with a tremor. His eyes opened. The three of us leaped up. We held onto his hands and his arms. He shivered once or twice and was gone.

Not long after my father's death, a nurse at the Friendship Home called me one afternoon and asked if I'd please come over as my mother was very agitated and confused and hard to handle.

I found my mother in a state of excitement and exaltation, trudging back and forth near a window in the lunchroom. Her short brown hair had never turned gray, and the soft skin of her face in the late afternoon light showed hardly a wrinkle. She had been eight years older than my dad and two inches taller. She remembered who I was, and she hastened to try to tell me what had happened. "Daddy came this morning," she said, smiling and eager. "He wanted to tell me all about a new kind of two-way radio he's found. It's just wonderful." She gestured vaguely with her fingers, shaping the air. "He said that he can talk to me on it from anywhere, and I can hear him. Even if he's as far away as Kansas, he can still talk to me. And I will hear him. No matter where he is, we can talk to each other."

I turned away to look out the window for a moment.

A few weeks later, photos of the two young elk entering their new home were posted in the local newspaper, along with information in the caption that they had been named John and Marge in honor of my parents.

Spaceships

ROGER LEVENSON was as down to earth as a guy could be. He was stolidly built, a tough, practical man who had survived a strange, agoraphobic mother plus persecution by mean little anti-semitical Christian boys at the private school he'd been sent to in lieu of familial care.

College was better, though his father was not pleased that his son ultimately preferred literature, music, and printing presses to the family furniture business in Maine. But Roger had already learned to be assertive, and he was not to be swayed by any arguments, especially financial ones.

In the Air Force, in World War II, he was involved in cryptography work.

He spent most of his adult life in the San Francisco area. He operated Tamalpais Press in Berkeley. He was frugal, even penny-pinching, out of necessity, as small letterpress printers insisting on exquisite typography do not attract the most lucrative jobs. He made a sleeping loft for himself in his shop. It was covered during the day in shipping boxes, in case any city inspector thought to investigate. He kept up a membership at the University pool and swam and showered there every day.

He taught book arts at the Bancroft Library on campus. One of his projects involved sending his students to comb through the stacks, looking for rare books unaccounted for. And his students always found several, to the consternation of librarians.

Roger knew the value of books. He visited his favorite used book shops almost every day, watching for the true bargains. He acquired in this manner over many years a substantive collection of books on Mozart, on book arts, and on Wagner. Mozart, in fact, was quite helpful in financing his retirement to Santa Barbara in his late sixties. As were the books on book arts. I inherited the Wagner collection.

When he discovered me and my two printing presses in Santa Barbara, he was able to continue what he most loved doing: teaching book arts to anyone who would sit down and listen.

He had belonged for many years to a group of private press printers, the Moxons, scattered around the Bay area and northern California. They had met monthly for years, sharing many charming keepsakes printed on the presses they kept polished in their living rooms, garages, or shops.

And so, one day, when I found Roger sitting under his beach umbrella on the Santa Barbara sands reading a copy of Shirley MacLaine's book, *Out on a Limb,* I wondered what was going through his exceptionally down-to-earth head. I had never detected in him the slightest interest in the spiritual world.

I dropped to my knees in the warm sand and peeked under his umbrella. "What in the world are YOU doing with that book?" I queried.

"I'm not a skeptic, though you might have assumed so," he said. "Doesn't mean this stuff is crazy. I've had my own experiences. That doesn't mean I care to talk about them."

He stuffed the book into his carryall bag with his shoes and socks. He put on his sunglasses.

Sensing something worth investigating, I burrowed deeper in the sand. Calculating that a detouring, roundabout attack was apt, I primed the pump. "Did I ever tell you, Roger, about Millie Warren, who used to work for me in Iowa? Her husband, before he died, used to own the salvage yard at Hamlin. She and her husband had one daughter. At the time Millie was working for me at the pottery in Audubon, her daughter was going to college in Cedar Falls. Can't remember her name. Anyway, she came home to visit Millie frequently on weekends and always prolonged the stay till late on Sunday to drive back to school.

"And then several Sunday visits in a row were concluded around noon, and the daughter drove back while it was still daylight. Millie didn't say anything but wondered what was going on.

"Finally, with some hesitation, the daughter told her

mother why. On one of the dark night trips home, as she was nearing Cedar Falls, she had taken her usual back roads short cut. Suddenly a light shone down into her car from directly above, following her, and she had a strange feeling that something was attempting to read her mind. So she began to sing out loud and drive as fast as she could. Just as she neared the outskirts of the city, the light swept suddenly away."

Roger raised his eyebrows and started to speak, but I shushed him.

"That's not all. Some time after that Millie one night was sitting in her living room watching TV when suddenly a bright light shone down through a window into the room and was moving around. Millie flopped down onto the floor and crawled on hands and knees out of range. There was no sound of a helicopter or anything."

Roger nodded and started to speak, but I interrupted him again.

"And then here's the really weird part. Millie and I were out at one of the festivals the historical society held at the county home park, and we were chatting with Everett Nelson, who used to own a hardware store in town. Somehow—maybe it was Halloween— we got onto the supernatural subject, and Millie told about her and her daughter's experiences.

"Everett then said, 'You know, my brother had a similar experience, but he never talks about it with anybody. He was driving home to his farm one night in his pickup and suddenly this light shone down into the cab and followed him. He couldn't see where it was coming from, but he barreled down the road, and he didn't slow down when he approached his driveway, but made a very fast, sudden turn into it. He looked up in time to see the light streak away across the sky.'

"Is that weird or what, Roger?"

"It's believable, frankly," he said. "I wouldn't say that if I hadn't seen one of those things myself. "

I scooted a little closer to him through the sand, and leaned in towards him.

"The Moxons were having a picnic meeting one summer, up by Columbia," he began. "We were high up, having a very pleasant dinner, chatting away, on a bright blue sky day. And then this flying saucer appeared. Clear as anything. It just sat there in the sky for maybe fifteen minutes, and we all just sat there and stared at it. Several of us were old Air Force guys, and we knew what planes looked like. It was no plane. Nobody said much, not then, and not much later, but we all knew what we'd seen. Or rather, we didn't know what we'd seen, but we'd seen something that was out of this world."

He took his sunglasses off and stared at me, raising his eyebrows. "It only takes one thing like that to open your mind to possibilities," he said. I nodded. And we didn't discuss it any further.

But that night I had perhaps the most wonderful dream

of my life. I was standing in the street on the south side of my Iowa hometown city square along with a number of other people. We had all looked up to watch something streak in a vast arc of light across the sky, then turn and swoop to a landing right in front of us on the street. We all stood there blinking as a misty fog around it slowly dissipated, revealing to our astonished eyes a large, white ice cream truck. There was no one in the cab. As the last of the mist melted away, we slowly edged closer. We could see writing on one of the doors, in fairly small print. Someone said softly, "I think we are watching a wonder!" I crept closer to the truck, and read aloud the fine print, "The wonder is watching you."

I bought my own copy of Shirley MacLaine.

A Visit to Iowa

D URING the seventeen years I lived and worked in Santa Barbara, my idea of a terrific vacation was to fly to my hometown of Audubon, in western Iowa, once or twice a year for a week's visit with my parents.

With one of those escapes from unreality on the horizon, I suggested to my friend Norbert Schiller, then in his mid-80s, that he might consider accompanying me. "We'll go to a Historical Society meeting in an old barn that's fixed up for a little theater."

Norbert's interest perked. "I could do a poetry reading," he said. The idea of a theater, any theater and any audience, had the old actor hooked.

I had paid $10 once to the Audubon County Historical Society to become a Lifetime Member. That elderly group would be delighted with a diversion, especially one that wouldn't involve history. That topic wears thin quickly in a rural area where not much has happened, other than the occasional flood, tornado, or circus. Historical Society meetings primarily involve lunch and coffee and worry about leaky museum roofs.

Norbert's much younger wife, Mary, was tickled with the idea of a week of freedom from cooking bounteous vegetarian meals for Norbert. "I'm going to go to Los Angeles," she confided. "Thanks for doing this!"

So I arranged the tickets. A quirk of timing decided that I was going to fly to Iowa a couple days before Norbert would. Mary would deliver him to Santa Barbara's airport, and I would retrieve him from Omaha's.

One evening a few days before our trip, Norbert came to my house for supper. Afterward we moved to the living room for our favorite entertainment: tape recording. We both enjoyed playing with my tape recorder, Norbert because he was performing, and me because I was capturing a beloved voice doing what it loved best.

I was always amazed at what came out of his long memory. The first time I'd turned on that tape recorder, he slowly extricated himself from the cheap futon couch and stood upright on the fuzzy carpet, weaving slightly. With a strong, sure voice and solely from memory he launched into the prologue to *Faust*, with histrionic gesture and with rapidly changing voices of God and the Devil in animated conversation. God's voice was low and ponderous, the Devil's lighter and humorously calculated. The voices interrupted each other, in an intense dialogue.

I never knew what curtain would go up when I flicked the tape recorder switch.

A little anxiety about the upcoming flight to Iowa seemed to be bothering Norbert that evening. He had a very Einsteinian look, as he had worried his hair into spikes sticking up at all angles. His bushy eyebrows drew down, increasing the rills of wrinkles between them.

A bewildered voice spoke softly to the recorder. "Oma... Omama...Omaha...I don't know...what if, what if no one comes to meet me here at the airport? I don't see Judy. So crowded. So many people, all in such a hurry. Oh, my. What do I do? Maybe that man—Sir, sir, do you know Judith Sood....Soodcliffah, ah, excuse me, excuse me. Sorry. Try another man...Mister, could you—'Leave me alone!!' Oh, my... Oh, dear, I'm all alone here. Where is Judy? Ah, who is this? (an oily female voice) 'May I help you, sir?' Oh, yes, oh yes, please. I am supposed to go to Odd—to Oddo—to the birds. 'Come with me, sir, I will help you, I am Salvation Army. Come, come'—oh, there's Judith—Here! Over here!"

There was no need of a Salvation Army rescue. I made sure I was at the airport way ahead of his flight.

Norbert had a fine week in Audubon. He watched fireflies every evening, flickering magic he hadn't seen since his youth in Germany. He performed. The small, politely attentive audience at the Historical Society's barn sat on hay bales and watched Norbert pace slowly back and forth while reciting the *Sorcerer's Apprentice* in German and then some of his own humorous poems in English. It wasn't every day that the Historical Society entertained a visiting German actor and poet.

On Saturday I took Norbert to what I considered the best theater in town, the local cattle auction at the sale barn near the fairgrounds. I loved to sit on the white painted bleachers in the steeply raked audience area and look down at the show. Cows would dash into the ring, lightly prodded by men with canes and whooping voices. The auctioneer would chant his magic numbers, and I would watch the audience to see if I could tell which farmer had winked or touched his ear in the rapid bidding. The cattle would come in one door, mill around a short while, then run out the other exit, leaving perhaps a plop or two behind.

Norbert and I took front row seats, right up by the metal fencing. The scent of cattle, dust, and of men in sweaty shirts hung in the warm, humid air. Norbert liked strong smells. But he seemed disconcerted by it all, the noise, the voices, and all the husky men in their farm caps and mud boots.

A bell rang, and a half dozen small black calves with knobby knees stumbled, confused, into the ring. Two men with canes hollered and whooped. One little calf ran directly toward us and jammed its wet, blue-grey nose through a space in the metal fencing. Its dark eyes—wide, white-rimmed, and frightened—stared at us.

Norbert reached out a pale, soft hand and touched the calf's nose. "Don't worry, little calf," he said, "I will never eat you."

We left before the second act.

The Journalist

Two of my high school classmates died in the flood of 1958. They got out of their car at the Hamlin highway intersection, five miles south of Audubon, Iowa, our home town. They were swept away downstream. Seventeen other people died in that spring flood, one of them a girl I played with as a child. One woman managed to hold onto a log for a nightmarish journey. She survived and told her story to the Presbyterian minister's tape recorder, for the Historical Society's records.

The day after the flood everyone in town was supposed to go to the City Hall and get shots. My father and I had been out in the middle of the night watching the dark water flow through the lumber yard, so we went for shots. It was pretty exciting.

Terry Barton, editor of the weekly *Audubon Advocate,* was there with his camera. It was probably the biggest story he'd ever had for a little country newspaper. Terry had salt and pepper hair, mowed really short. He always wore a bow tie, and he lisped just a little.

He walked up to me and said, "I need to hire you for a few days, until we get this paper out. Come on down to the office when you're through."

He knew me only slightly. I was editor of the high school's little newspaper and wrote most of it. He printed it for the school. I think he had especially liked the April Fool edition I had just written, with my tongue in my cheek.

I went down to the newspaper office, which was in the building where the Isis movie theater used to be. Terry's office was up in the projection room. Notes and copy went up and down to the projection window in a cardboard box on a string. I loved the clicking and clacking of typewriters and linotypes and the rhythmic thumping of the big sheet-fed press near the back of the building.

My dire assignment, my first paid job—if I don't count mending books at the library for fifty cents an hour—was to call all the families of the nineteen who had drowned.

"Just use the obit form and get all the correct name spellings, birth dates, family relatives, all the vital statistics," Terry said. "Then you write a short obituary for each one. Just straight facts. No emotions."

That was the front page of the *Audubon Advocate* that week.

When I graduated and went to the University of Iowa in Iowa City, Terry would hire me in the summers to write and photograph stories for the big Beef Edition of the paper. That was when the raising of beef cattle was a really big deal in western Iowa, and the Audubon Jaycees built a 30 ft. high Hereford bull out of steel and concrete at the edge of town. That golden calf is still there, with its blue eyes and eyelashes, although the beef industry and the Chicago and Omaha stockyards are long gone.

Preparing the Beef Edition was definitely journalism on the hoof. Terry would give me a list of names of farmers to interview, and I would take it from there. The first time I went out for an interview, he handed me a box camera to take with me. I had no idea how to use it as it involved lens settings. Terry looked at the sky, made a lens setting, and just said, "Don't change that." I drove the newspaper's old station wagon out to a farm, interviewed the farmer, and took several pictures of him posing with some of his black Angus cattle.

When I got back to the news office, I handed the camera to Terry. He wound it up, his brow wrinkling, and then announced to the entire office staff, with a couple cuss words I wasn't used to hearing, "Who forgot to put film in this goddamned camera?"

I went back out to the farm with film in the camera and repeated the photos. The farmer was more amused than anything else. I remember asking him at some point why he liked farming. He answered, "It's the gamble of it. The risk of trying to do something that's at the mercy of weather, disease, markets. You never know what's going to happen."

On one of the interviews I was supposed to talk to a prominent and rather crusty old guy, Nick Jensen, who owned several farms. I met him at one place, but he was busy and wanted to go over to another farm first and told me to follow him. I was driving the old station wagon. He was one heck of a fast country driver. He just roared down those dusty gravel roads. Suddenly, as he zipped up the road toward the crest of a hill, a roof appeared directly over the road. A house was being moved right down the middle. Nick never even slowed. He just swerved down into the grassy ditch on the right and drove past the oncoming house. I followed him into the ditch and back onto the road, gravel spinning, then on to his farm and the interview, which, I believe, was on the short side.

Terry Barton introduced me to journalism, seat of the pants variety, and even better, he introduced me to wild and fearless creative writing. It was while I was still in high school, typing my assignments carefully on the Royal Portable typewriter my parents had given me when I graduated from eighth grade. I had correction paper slips and correction fluid, and I would write my assignments first in pencil and then neatly type them on the Royal. I thought of it more as a printing device than a composition tool.

But one night I went with my parents to the local Home Show in the high school gym. Audubon businesses had booths there and touted their wares. A big crowd of local people were milling around, there not being much else in town to do, and there was even a little air of excitement.

I spotted some shelves displaying Smith Corona typewriters, which Terry sold at the newspaper office. But I couldn't see Terry for all the people thronged around his booth. I got in line and gradually pushed forward. Finally I could see that Terry was seated at a rickety little typewriter table out in the aisle in front of his booth, with a Smith Corona portable, and his fingers were flying. He seemed oblivious of the people who were nudging each other to get a better look over his shoulder at what he was typing, but they were laughing and giggling. I was just as curious, and when I finally won a position to see over his shoulder and read what he was typing at a furious clacking rate, I, too, started to giggle.

"hi judy judy judy," he was typing, "this is stream of consciousness typewriting the only way to go go go up to the heights and down to the depths and how's your mom and dad these days and don't forget we don't go gently into that deep good night we just keep typing typing typing."

Well, something like that.

I went home and put a piece of paper in my Royal Portable, and just started typing.

Old Dogs

An enormous lilac bush grew in Art and Nellie's front yard, somewhat obscuring the old grey farmhouse, which had seen no paint in recent years, if any, ever. Today, all is gone, the scent of lilacs wafted far away, nothing left of the house, the trees, the bushes, the daylilies that didn't need tending, the outhouse, all gone. Nothing now but pasture. If an archeologist happened to dig there someday, for no particular reason, he might turn up, amid the arrowheads, a Prince Albert tobacco can or rusty rings from horse harness.

My parents' woodland acreage was just down the gravel road from Art Winder's gate, and Dad befriended Art and Nellie from the start. The 54 acres of trees and wildflowers were my father's way of de-stressing from being a 24-hour-a-day country veterinarian in western Iowa. There was no telephone in the cabin hidden up a hill, beyond the pond, amid the hickory trees.

For some reason, my father hankered after pine trees.

He grew up in flatland Kansas, and possibly a vacation with mom and my squabbling little sister and me in Colorado marked pine trees for him as serene, quiet, and restful. And maybe he just decided to make a big deal of planting a lot of pines because he knew that Art Winder still had a pair of plowhorses.

My father had, at that time in the early 1950s, a wind-up Keystone movie camera. My mother managed to catch a few seconds in black and white of Art's big horses and behind them my dad with the reins slung over his shoulders, hanging tightly on to the plow while leaning back and trotting his boots along at a mighty fine pace. Mom and my sister and me followed along later, thrusting the pine seedlings into the plowed furrow.

Most of the pines died, despite a lot of watering and concern, but one group did survive. Decades later, it always seemed like entering another world to walk into that pine grove. No grass, no wildflowers, no weeds, just soft brown needles on the ground, a strangely silent, meditative space with the everpresent Iowa winds reduced to soft whisperings. The resting place for my father's and mother's ashes.

It was a treat for my sister and me to visit the Winders. My parents would stop the car at their mailbox, and we'd run up the weedy path to the porch, which was laden with boxes and buckets and old tools. A honeysuckle vine, healthy and heavy, weighed down the porch roof.

Art's three hounds would reach us first, shaking their

rear ends off, jumping up for kisses. Art would shamble out the screen door, his old knees bowed a bit, his chest still broad, a shock of white hair falling across his wide forehead. Nellie would be right behind him, a heavy stocky woman in a large cotton dress, with bare legs in lace up work shoes. She had short, straight grey hair, an ugly big nose, and she breathed heavily as she walked, tipping from side to side. I found it hard to imagine how Art had ever fallen in love with her.

We'd always be invited to come inside and set awhile. This was an adventure that we loved to share with unsuspecting young friends. We first entered the kitchen. Right in front of us was a big round table, stacked about two feet high with old pots and pans, cereal boxes, jars empty but unwashed, and empty food cans. Once we caught Art eating lunch from a tin pie pan, half on, half off the table, there being no room for the entire plate.

"Best breakfast I ever had," he said, waving a large hand over the mountain on the table, "was the summer when the honeybees made a hive right up there in the attic. We could just hold our biscuits out and catch that honey dripping down. Nothin' better."

He and Nellie normally entertained in the living room, reached through a corridor of newspapers stacked on chairs. Nellie wrote the local rural gossip column for the Guthrie Center paper and apparently had saved every issue for a great many years. Inside the living room, we would either have to stand or remove a stack of papers from a chair to sit down.

My parents would sit, but my sister and I and our friends from town would stand up so as to get closer to Art. He always engaged us in conversation.

"What's your name?" he'd ask the stranger. Then, "What's your politics?" Clear answers to that one were to be avoided, in the hopes he'd proceed directly to question number three: "Can yeh dance?" Our friends had been coached to say "Yes," and that would bring the old fiddle out of its case. The old fingers, flattened on the tips from a lifetime of fiddling, would seek their accustomed places, and the dance tunes would leap forth.

There really wasn't enough space for dancing, but we'd always jump around and twirl and laugh, enough to keep Art playing for a good lively while.

My mother realized one day that Art's memory was failing, and she asked him if he'd write down his memoirs for her. He actually did that, handwritten on two sides of one sheet of paper, a stream of images that poured forth from his past: pretty women, a petite gloved hand in his, driving cattle across the plains into Canada, staying overnight at a hospitable sod house, sleeping with the pretty daughter in the same bed with a bundling board between them but hands that crossed the barrier, following Indian families moving camp with horses and travois, playing the fiddle for dances, dancing with a woman in a red dress, and on and on. I knew then that Nellie must have been pretty in her salad days, as Art was a romantic fellow then, with an eye for loveliness.

Around the time I was away in college, my parents became increasingly worried about the old couple's ability to care for themselves, especially in winter. Their son in Washington state readily agreed to let my parents be official guardians. The sad thing they knew they had to do was to move Art and Nellie to the Friendship Home. It was for their own good. Nellie had a fine time at the nursing home, with lots of people to socialize with. Art, however, was sullen and depressed. He felt betrayed. He missed his dogs and the country. He wasn't interested in getting out his fiddle.

During my Christmas break one year Mom and Dad brought Art and Nellie over to our small house for dinner. Afterwards, everyone but Art sat around the kitchen table drinking home-canned grape juice and playing cards. Art wouldn't budge from the living room chair. I went in and sat by him.

He talked to me of the "mud baby" I'd made out of clay in the ditch by the acreage one summer, nearly life size. "I'd watch the cars put on their brakes and back up," he said, "they couldn't figure out what that was."

I told him how much I liked the memoirs he'd written, and I commented on the number of pretty ladies he'd known in those days. He turned to glance toward the kitchen group, who were laughing and chatting, then he said, in a lowered voice, "I'll tell you my secret." He leaned toward me and whispered, "Cocoa butter. You just put a little in a can lid on the stove, melt it. It works really good. In all those years Nellie and I only had one child."

I thanked him and said I was really glad to know it.

Some months later my mother called me in the dormitory at Iowa City to tell me that Art had died. The moment she said that, I saw Art's dogs all leaping up, paws to his chest, tongues licking his grizzled chin.

Never did try the cocoa butter. But I appreciated the advice.

The Trial

THE PHONE RANG. He did not identify himself, knowing full well I would know his voice even after years had passed. Our last conversation, in his Talbot-Carlson office in Iowa, was cold and silent on his part, arrogant and giddy on mine, as I left his employment—and friendship—in what I'd hoped was a blaze of independent glory.

He could be boot shaking on the phone. Anyone who called his office number got no pleasantries, just "TAL-BOT!" Loud, fast and no nonsense.

And now that voice from Iowa thrust through my Santa Barbara phone. "Did you ever see a Perry Mason show?" he began, and I stuttered, "Uh, yeah, I guess so."

He pressed on. "Whenever Perry was in court and got into trouble, he brought in a secret witness. I'd like you to be my secret witness."

After a fractional second of stunned silence on my part, he continued, "And I'll pay your airfare home so you can visit your parents. But you have to stay out of sight until I tell you to show up at the courthouse."

"Tully," I said, "Umm, this sounds like fun. Yes, I'll come back to Audubon. What's the deal?"

He explained.

Although Talbot-Carlson, Inc., his company, supplied free choice minerals for cattle, he had also acquired another local corporation, Emmert Manufacturing. It produced hog confinement buildings, some of the earliest ones experimented with in the 1970s.

At the time that I was creating advertising for Tully's companies in those years, Emmert Andersen was experimenting with a confinement building that would hold several hundred small pigs in a series of pens. There was an automatic feeding system and, most wondrous, two giant toilet tanks of water at one end which would each, on timed occasions, flush the pig poop down a concrete gulley running along the sides of the building and outside to a pond. Emmert initially adjusted the water flow by dropping concrete blocks into the big fiberglas tanks.

Now, how do you design a small, crowded, concrete-floored pig pen that will restrict poop to a gutter and not mix it into the sleeping and eating area? Emmert had relied on someone's understanding of pig psychology. Apparently, the piggies like to chat with other piglets, not while lunching, but while doing pig business. So the sleeping and eating area was fenced with sheets of fiberglas that were opaque.

The only areas that featured open wire fencing were over the gutter. That's where the pigs could chat, snout to snout, with neighbors in the next pens. And every hour or so, the water would flow. It actually worked fairly well.

As soon as the bugs were worked out, or nearly so, Tully and Emmert started selling Pig Pokes right and left. Land prices were high. Loans were easy to get. Happy days, smiling farmers.

I designed color brochures for the buildings, as well as black and white ads for hog industry publications. Among other things, I wrote up a folksy newsletter to hand out to dealers and farmers. It featured an interview with the young and progressive owner of one of the very first Pig Pokes.

Time passed rapidly. I quit in the mid 1970s and moved to California in 1978. In the early 1980s the bottom fell out of farming in the Midwest. Farmers went bankrupt. Agricultural businesses like Tully's struggled to stay alive. The young farmer with the Pig Poke was in financial straits. According to Tully, the young man saw an opportunity to gain some time and some cash, and he sued Talbot Carlson, Inc. His claim was that the Pig Poke building was defective, that hundreds of his pigs had died because of its design defects, and he wanted thousands of dollars in recompense.

"But I know," said Tully, "that those pigs died because he stuffed way too many of them into that building. Way more than what we had recommended. They died because of the farmer's greed.

"You're my secret witness," he said. "We found a newsletter you'd written about that particular farmer and the hog buildings. You quoted him in black and white stating the number of pigs he was putting in the building. Way too many.

"I'm not likely to win this suit, but I know who's in the wrong and intend to prove it. We're entering that newsletter as evidence for our side, and I'd like to spring you at the right moment to verify that you wrote it and he said it. "

This was definitely too much fun to miss. My past anger at Tully had long since faded away, so I flew back to Iowa delighted to play in his game once again.

I hid out at my parents' house. They were amused, and we had a pleasant time together waiting for the trial to move forward. Then Tully called one night and said to show up at 10:00 the next morning.

I entered the Audubon County courthouse court room to find it filled with men, farmers who looked quizzically at me. Tully's attorney presented the newsletter information, and just like on the Perry Mason show, they called me to the stand as the secret witness. They asked me if I'd written the material and I had. The judge seemed to need to justify a little more information and asked me how big the pigs were that I'd seen the day I'd been on the farm in question. A real farmer would have answered that question, I think, in pounds, but I just held my hands out to show how big a little pig was. That created a titter of laughter through the audience. And then I could step down and that was that.

Tully told me to go to his daughter's western shop on the highway and pick out some western pants, a shirt, and a belt, as a thank you.

A few weeks later he phoned me in Santa Barbara. "I would never have believed it," he said, "but I won the case. I think your presence somehow was the clincher. It made everybody laugh and lighten up, and we won. Come see me next time you're in Audubon."

The next year on my annual home visit, I think I phoned him and said hello, but I didn't have time to meet. He reprimanded me. The next year he picked me up in his truck and took me to lunch in Exira, ten miles down the highway. He had a salad, not his usual fare. Our old friendship, which had almost strayed beyond the edge a couple times, was restored. As we left, closing the restaurant door behind us, he caught my arm, pulled me to him, and kissed me hard, once, on the mouth.

"Don't forget me," he said. "Come see me when you come back again. I won't be here forever, you know."

I didn't, of course, believe him. He had a heart attack and died two months later.

The Lumber Yard

THE LIFE OF A SALESMAN is fraught with rejection. It was my summer job in Audubon, Iowa, my home town, between college exits and entrances. I was attempting to sell ads for the Audubon newspaper's annual Beef Edition. Beef cattle were a successful rural industry in those days, the early 1960s, and this special edition would contain feature stories about local cattle feeders, which I would write, and should also contain many columns and pages of advertising from feed stores, implement dealers, local restaurants, and all businesses profiting from cattle. The advertising was the point of putting out such an edition.

On this particular day, a hot, humid July day that I had spent bouncing around the small towns of the county in an unairconditioned VW Beetle, I hadn't sold one inch of advertising.

I was discouraged. I was sweating. I didn't mind writing stories about cows, but I hated pitching ads, asking businessmen to buy something that to me was of questionable value.

I was not born to be an advertising salesman. But I was being paid to do it.

The next little town on Highway 71 was Brayton, a bothersome little slow-down on the road, its half a block of store fronts nearly dead or dying.

But there was a lumber yard between Main Street and the next corn field, with concrete blocks, creosoted posts, wire fencing scattered around the building, interspersed with green foxtails and young burdock, innocuous at this stage. Ignored until fall, their fiendish burrs would tangle the fur of wandering dogs and cats.

I entered the office, a large room with a high long counter, stacked here and there with thick catalogs of everything from windows to paint sprayers, along with piles of order sheets, in some disorder. The counter was old and wooden, worn and bruised about the edges.

A small, elderly man with a round head and very little hair sat on a high wooden chair behind the far side of the counter. When he saw me, he rolled his chair briskly along the counter until he faced me. I noticed that his shoulders sloped, one higher than the other. A pair of aluminum crutches leaned against a table in the room I could see behind him, the angled kind that fit against the forearm.

I was not happy, as I knew that I had to ask this man for an ad. No one else was in the building. Tendrils of my hair were sticking to my sweaty forehead. I frowned.

The man tilted his head to one side and looked at me

rather benignly, I thought, through his wire-rimmed glasses. He smiled, and I felt a sudden warmth that wasn't related to the July sun. "What can I do for you, my dear," he said, raising his gray eyebrows slightly.

Something about him opened a door in my heart. I started to cry. He tilted his head to the other side and waited silently for me to speak.

"I'm selling ads for the Audubon paper's beef edition," I managed to say, rubbing out the tears, "and I haven't sold any today and I hate selling ads. I hate it. There. That's how I feel. Pretty down."

"I usually don't buy an ad in the paper," he said, and my eyes flitted toward the doorway. "I don't buy ads because they're never done well. Just stock photos and stock language. But if you would like to come up with something original just for my business, something different, I'll buy a quarter page."

I gulped, and my eyes widened. "I'll be happy to dream up something for you," I said. "I like to write, and I like writing ads, among other things. Just don't like selling them. I'll design an ad for you."

He nodded, with a slight smile shadowing his round moon face. "How old are you?" he asked, as I started, somewhat reluctantly, to turn toward the door. "You must be about my nephew's age."

"I'll be a sophomore at the University of Iowa this fall," I said, not moving. "Where's your nephew?"

"He's just gone into basic training in Florida," he said. "He's as close to me as my own child. I really miss him."

"Are you afraid he'll get hurt?" I asked.

"I would know if he was injured," he said. "Right here." And he put his right hand on the left side of his abdomen, where his gray trousers bunched up.

"What do you mean?" I said.

Lowering his voice as if there were some secrets afoot, he said, "I always know in my body how the people who are closest to me are feeling. If my wife at home was unhappy or ill, I would feel it here," and he moved his hand just above his belt.

I wrinkled my forehead. "How do you do that?"

He said, "It's like a radio. I'm a receiver. My nephew, my wife, my brother, they're each on a different frequency of radio waves, and I can always tell when something's wrong. I'll go home at night and ask my wife what was bothering her at 11 o'clock, and she'll tell me that she cut her finger slicing onions or she heard a really sad story and was crying. They all know that I can read them that way. If my wife was in real bad pain, I would feel it and go to her. I can't go to my nephew, if he is wounded, but I will be the first to know."

I would not say that there was a visible radiance around this man, but there was something that came forth from him that was gently electrifying to my entire being. I drove home to Audubon in a state of high happiness. I woke up the next morning with the design of the lumber yard ad in my head and I drew a picture of a lively calf in black ink to illustrate it.

The ad ran. I went back to school.

I never saw him again.

Vocabulary

J was marooned in Hagen, Germany, in a girls school in 1967, a victim of my own over-confidence in the minuscule amount of German language I actually could operate. Most of my vocabulary was hiked off classical lieder records. In the first day at the school I referred to "Backen," which I thought, from the lieder of only a hundred or so years ago, meant cheeks. Well, it did, but not the ones on your face. I'm sure now that during the months I was there, I must have caused a lot of laughter among the teachers, mostly behind my back. . . or cheeks.

When I was in college at the University of Iowa, I had met a young grad student in my dorm who was from Germany. When she found that a small town Iowa girl actually liked German poetry and lieder, she gave me the address of one of her teachers in Hagen. Always game for an adventure in human relations, I wrote a letter to Hildegarde Putz in my cribbed-from-the-classics vocabulary, sans grammar.

Frau Putz answered me in English in charming fashion, sent me exquisite photos she had taken of beech trees in uncommon light, and, being of an impressionable nature, naturally I fell in love with her and her photos. She arranged for me to come live with her and be an exchange English teacher for one school year.

The romantic haze wore off real fast. I sat in some of Putz' English classes and watched her frighten students into paralysis. She was a small, lithe woman with short, curly grey hair. When a student, standing, couldn't answer the question or repeat a memorized English paragraph, Putz would inhale sharply, eyes glittering, like a puffer fish inflating. "Idiot!" she would hiss, piercing whatever small balloon of self-confidence yet remained in the poor kid. Parents actually sued her.

I didn't last too long at her apartment. If I came softly into a room and surprised her, she would demand, "For heaven's sake, make some noise when you enter." If I then clumped my shoes a little as I came through the door, she would angrily snap, "Don't make so much noise!"

A couple of the other teachers at the school rescued me from Putz and found me a small apartment with a shared bath. It was near a cemetery and had to be evacuated once when an American bomb was found in a newly dug grave.

One of the kind teachers, Herr Schmidt, took pity on me and rather adopted me for the rest of the school year. He would frequently take me home to the apartment he shared with his wife and little girl and feed me. We'd all watch the television together or listen to avantgarde dissonant classical music that I didn't like but wasn't about to say so.

I found the television fascinating because TV commercials, rather than interrupt programs every 15 minutes as I was used to, were all grouped together for an hour at 6:00 pm. They were intensely watched because of some adorable little Mainzlmännchen, funny little animated dwarves, who would zip into action between commercials, do a trick, giggle, and disappear until the end of the next commercial. It seemed to me a very enlightened way of handling advertisements.

Sometimes the four of us went for walks in the woods on well-traveled paths, dressed in Sunday clothes. We'd meet well-dressed couples trundling baby carriages in the midst of the forest. One day, Lili, the nine-year-old daughter, went scampering off amid the pine trees, as youngsters as wont to do. But the reaction of Herr and Frau Schmidt was distressing. They called the child back to the path in the sternest of language, and gave her a paddling when she got there. She was told to stay on the path, no running about.

I was perturbed. Why would a child's natural instincts to explore be so rudely curbed? Herr Schmidt explained to me that there were still landmines in the forest, and no one knew where they were, an everpresent, lurking danger.

Sometimes while Frau Schmidt was cooking dinner, Herr Schmidt would take me for a short walk into the woods along a pretty stream. I was young and vulnerable and, apparently, of a certain charm, because one day, at the end of the trail, he took my shoulders in his hands and kissed me.

At this point, he was my only close friend in Germany, and I was lonely and isolated by my slowness in learning German, sitting through dinner parties not understanding a single joke when all the other teachers were laughing heartily.

I was also declared useless as a teacher and was only used for babysitting classes when teachers were ill. The unforgivable problem was that I unfortunately had an American accent. The children were supposed to learn English with a British accent. Choose-day, not Toos-day.

So I returned the kiss. This was the era of the sexual revolution, and I was as free as males always had been to taste forbidden fruits, and I did, with no apologies or second thoughts at the time.

After some months of stolen kisses, Herr Schmidt's wife and daughter went away for several days to visit relatives. He stayed behind, looking forward to a tryst with me.

So. After dinner and preliminaries, we climbed into the big double bed which was actually two beds in one frame, a typical German marriage bed. We undressed each other partially, and I had a vocabulary lesson on body parts. I found the German words for nipples especially gross: Brustwartze or breast-warts. And pubic hair was Schamhaare or shame-hair. I cringed at the implications.

But I was along for the ride. Just when I thought we were

going to have a go at it, Herr Schmidt pulled away. Smoothing his dark hair over his broad and balding forehead, he said softly to me, "Have you ever been afraid?"

"Well, sure, I guess," I said, libido cooling rapidly. "Um, scarey movies, being in my parents' creaky old house alone at night. Walking home alone in Chicago at night. That's about it."

"No," he reiterated. "I mean have you ever been so frightened that you could not move, could not do anything."

"No," I said.

"All Germans have," he said.

He buttoned his shirt. "I can't do this," he said. "My wife and I were refugees from the East. We met while we were escaping, walking and walking for miles. We helped each other, we stood by each other, we survived. We're not in love, maybe we never were. But still, I can't do this and think of her and all we've been through together."

I buttoned my clothes up, too.

The kisses stopped, though the friendship and family visits continued. About the time that I was leaving for America, Herr Schmidt was planning a vacation in Italy—teachers in Germany get a lot of vacation time—and he said he would stay in touch.

Back in the States a few weeks later I received a black-edged note from his wife that he had died of a brain tumor in Italy.

Uncle John

THE BEST DOGGONE BREAKFAST I ever ate and by far the best garbage disposal I ever saw was way down in southeast Missouri Ozarks, in my mother's home territory.

Mom was born in a log cabin in the woods and grew up with three ornery brothers who played gleefully with rattlesnakes and copperheads. Plus a grandmother, sister, mother, and baby brother who all died of consumption, as they called tuberculosis then, in the early 1900s.

When the ornery brothers grew up, Charles went to work in a Tennessee munitions factory and stayed there. Will went to work in an Ozark lumber mill. The third one, John McVicker was a farmer. At the time my family used to go visit him, John lived alone in the old, two-story, white clapboard farmhouse in the backwoods that his father had bought or built for the family after giving up on log cabin life. Steep front steps lead us directly to the second floor, where the kitchen, living room, and bedrooms were located. Whatever occupied the ground floor level was a mystery.

When my parents, my sister, and I stayed overnight at Uncle John's one summer, Juanita and I had a room to ourselves with two metal bedsteads and tired mattresses. We were worn out from the long drive south from Iowa, but sleep was difficult to achieve. After talking softly about the day's events and being on the verge of dropping off to sleep, a little scratching sound raised our eyelids. "What's that?" my sister said, sitting up.

"I don't know," I answered. "Must be mice."

As the night deepened, the rustling sounds increased. Within the walls there were scurryings from one side of the room to the other. There would be a pause, silence, then furious scurryings and even some squeaking.

"They make a lot of noise," I whispered. "They must be rats."

This was not comforting to my little sister, who'd once been bitten by a rat that terrorized our Audubon, Iowa, household for one night until my father cornered the creature and smashed it to death with a baseball bat. Lucky for her it wasn't rabid. My veterinarian father sent the rat's head to a lab in Ames to certify its health and my sister's escape from rabies shots.

We were glad when the sun came up and the things in the walls quieted down.

Juanita and I, yawning but not complaining, joined our parents and Uncle John in the kitchen. They were sitting around the old wooden table, drinking coffee and chatting away about all the assorted relatives and classmates Mom still kept tabs on. When Juanita and I settled into chairs at the table, Uncle John said he was ready to make breakfast for us all. He had the wood range going and two or three cast iron skillets at the ready.

Although he raised hogs that ran wild in the woods, he peeled off a whole package of store bought bacon, laying the strips in two skillets. He had a big coffee can full of fresh eggs from his hens at the side, ready to plunge their contents into the bubbling bacon grease when the succulent strips shriveled up and were lifted out with a fork.

But before he started the eggs, he did something I'd never seen before. He introduced us all to modern, high-tech biscuit making. He took a round canister from his refrigerator and whacked the thing over the back of the nearest empty chair. The cardboard split, and white, already formed, wet biscuits pushed themselves outward, white pillows swelling larger and larger as Uncle John extracted them from the can. He put them quickly in the oven, got out the butter and jam, cracked the eggs in the grease. It was one of those once in a lifetime breakfasts, bacon grease and biscuits at their best.

But the topper was yet to come. We were patting our stomachs and starting to talk about helping with the dishes. Uncle John cleared the table. There was a closed door flanked by two open windows at the back kitchen wall. I hadn't really paid attention to that door. But Uncle John now went over to it with a plate piled with the remains of too many biscuits and too much bacon fat. He opened the upper part of what I now realized was a Dutch door, and the morning sun streamed in.

Uncle John leaned over the half door, scraped the plates into the atmosphere, and let loose with a loud "Soooooooeeeee."

I hurried to the door and peered out. From our second story height, the food scraps had fallen to the ground below. Two hairy-backed, blackish hogs came running on neat little hooves to the garbage heap. It was gone in an instant, with considerable grunting and huffing.

I've never owned a garbage disposal that could compare with Uncle John's.

The Star

SLIP OFF THE SAGGING rubber band from the packet of plastic cards in clear plastic pockets, the residence of my credit cards, and shake them all out. Two vital credit cards, drivers license, a bank card for ATMs, Social Security card, miniature birth certificate, AAA, AARP, insurance, Medicare, they all fan out across the table.

But tucked in between these necessities of identified life or death, are a few souvenirs, credit card size.

I pick up a little photograph of Sandy standing tall next to her lifelong hero, Roy Rogers, a year before his death, in his electric cart, in his California museum, in a white cowboy hat. And this one is my reader's card for the Huntington Library in Pasadena, with several dates handwritten on it from 1985 to 1993, when I visited there with Roger Levenson. Now expired from disuse, I suppose. And then there's this smudgy white card: "Judith Ann Sutcliffe has passed a written examination in the Public Boating Course given by this squadron under the auspices of the United

States Power Squadrons. Santa Barbara, May 1991," and someone's signature.

I'd flunk that exam today, I'm sure. But I passed it with flying colors back then, and I actually took another squadron class in navigation, at Willie Craig's urging. He wanted me to know what I was doing if I sailed with him on his 30 ft. fiberglas tub. So I did learn some of the basic things about sailing in the Pacific Ocean. You'll die in 15 minutes if you fall out of the boat, especially useful knowledge for guys who stumble to the railing in the middle of the night to pee or throw up. The water's cold. And you don't have to worry about lightning on the Pacific, even though you have to know the answers to lightning questions to pass the test.

I kind of liked the navigation part which involved rulers and sea maps and calculations. It was an organized way of guessing where the hell you were. Willie, who took the classes with me, got into arguments with the teacher over why sailors today should bother doing sun or star sightings and arcane calculations with ancient equipment now extinct in the wake of new GPS technology.

Willie's boat was blue, a very pretty light, dusty blue. We had a hard time deciding on a name, but I finally painted our choice on the side: Swing Dancer. Willie was a good swing dancer, had been since he was a youngster skipping school on Staten Island to hang out around Times Square, watching the dancers and picking up the steps. We met at a dance in Santa Barbara at a time when he'd just bought a sailboat from the

1960s and had it perched upright in Ventura Harbor drydock, 30 miles south of Santa Barbara, where I lived.

He tore everything out of it, cleaned it all up, and then put back what he considered the necessities. A chemical toilet was not one of them. "The damn things stink," he said. "It was the first thing I got rid of." It was replaced by a five gallon bucket with a toilet seat on top and by plastic detergent jugs with wide mouths and screw lids. The ocean was wide and deep, and human waste organic. I think that was his rationale.

So, with a lot of cabbage, onions, apples, tin cans and no refrigerator, we went to sea. There was a cute little two-burner stove in the galley that would rock back and forth the opposite way the boat rocked, so at least in mild waters, the tea kettle would stay put over a propane flame.

Willie's dreams were large. "I want to be the oldest man to circumnavigate the globe," he'd say. He had a few books on board, and they were all stories of sailing adventures. He intended, thank goodness, to do that alone. He'd initially taken the boat out in storms to see how the sails he'd designed would work. He'd limp back in with the sails ripped and rework the whole thing. He had a lot of fun for a frugal guy in his late sixties, living on Social Security and a little savings.

If you stand on shore in Santa Barbara and look out to sea, there's a long range of bumps at the horizon. These are the Channel Islands. Santa Cruz Island was big enough for a cattle ranch and a tiny Catholic chapel. A Chumash Indian woman was abandoned on another island and lived there alone for years before someone thought about rescuing her. A little elephant lived on one island, a baby mastodon, whose bones are in the Natural History Museum along with questions as to how he got out there.

There are about twenty-five miles of ocean between Santa Barbara or Ventura and the islands. Somewhere in between mainland and islands is a shipping lane that huge container ships follow. On a clear day, the ships are easy to see, and you have enough time to paddle out of the way. They're like locomotives. They're fast and they don't have brakes. But in the fog, which can arise on what had appeared to be a clear day, you can only guess where those great big lunkers are located. It's scarey. You pay careful attention to the maps and where you think you are and where the shipping channel is marked. And you keep really quiet and listen. You might be able to hear another small sailboat, with a bell or occasional horn toot, and escape a bump, but all you'd hear if a big ship suddenly appeared starboard would be a death knell.

Except for the container ships, crossing the channel on a pretty summer day was great fun for a Midwest landlubber like me. "Here," Willie said the first day we went out."You steer." And he handed me the tiller. I had no time to protest. "Just watch the compass here and keep her on track." He was buckling a rope around his waist and climbing forward like a monkey, quick and sure, in order to change something about the sails. Power squadron class or not, I never did quite understand what he did with the sails. He always knew where the wind was coming from, from the very slightest indications. "See that little ripple out there?" he'd say. "Wind's changing." And then he'd fuss with the sails.

The boat didn't go very fast, it was not built for speed. But it was a heavy old tub and not about to fall over in a swift breeze. I did feel secure about that part. I wondered if I would get seasick, but Willie handed me little packets of saltine crackers. "Just don't go below," he said. "Keep your eyes on the horizon and nibble at the crackers. You won't get seasick." And he was right.

We made the trip to the islands several times. The best part was the dolphins. They would swim right alongside the boat, especially near the front, I mean, the bow. Willie tied the rope around me once and let me climb way up front and lay down to watch the dolphins leaping just inches away.

When we reached the islands after several hours of slow sailing, we would anchor along the coast of Santa Cruz. You weren't allowed on the islands, but you could anchor nearby. Anchoring was a major skill because the coast was rocky and there were few quiet bays. Most sailboats put out two anchors and paid close attention to them.

We got involved in cooking supper one night on the south end of Santa Cruz and didn't pay attention. I was looking out a little window. "Willie, I think those rocks are getting closer!" He leaped up the ladder to check his anchors, and I followed. We were indeed drifting slowly toward a wall of big jagged rocks.

"I don't think there's time to reset the anchors," he frowned. "The only thing we can do is head back out to sea." He started up the little diesel, pulled in the anchors, and while I held my breath, he managed to steer us clear of the rocks and back out into open water. The sun had just gone down, leaving a slight glow all around the horizon. Darkness would be upon us very quickly.

We were a safe distance from the island now and heading north along the island's east coast. Finding a safe place to anchor in the settling dark was going to be difficult.

The little diesel pushed the boat slowly forward. A wind had come up, and white caps were visible in what little light Swing Dancer threw to the water.

And then Willie said, "I hate to tell you this, but I'm getting seasick." He looked pale. "You're going to have to take over until I can maneuver," he said. "Go down and look at the chart. There's a bay where there's a wharf, I think, about half way up the island. Figure out the compass direction, and then come back up here and steer. And hurry."

I went below and used, for once, what I'd learned in Power Squadron classes. I figured out the compass direction, not that it was a very difficult task, but we were going to be sailing very shortly in pitch darkness, and what we didn't want to do was aim the wrong direction and crash on the rocks.

Back on deck, I took the tiller and watched the compass. "Look for a star in the same direction," Willie said in a faint voice. He was sitting on a bench and looked totally drained. I had never seen him like this, and gradually, as I stood, legs apart, leaning into the tiller, I grew angry at him. Why did he fall apart in an emergency? I'm just the passenger. I've never done this before. What if I run us on the rocks? Why can't he do this? He's the strong one. He's the captain.

I calmed down eventually, as it was a very long night. Willie was as limp as a doll that had come unstuffed. I watched the compass, and I found a bright star to head toward. The little five horsepower diesel pushed us through the heaving ocean, slow but sure. This went on for literally hours. Willie dozed off. I just kept watching that star, mesmerized, and sleepy myself. It seemed to get brighter and brighter.

"Willie, I think you better wake up," I called, now a little worried because the star was wobbling slightly, or I was. He jumped up. He'd sloughed off the seasickness, and he quickly took the tiller.

"You did a good job," he said. "Better than you know. That's not a star. At least not the one that's wobbling. It's a boat in the harbor. It's exactly where we want to be."

The sea was calmer now as we approached the island's best harbor, where the cattle boats moored. Somehow during the long night the star had morphed into a light on the mast of a cattle boat. We were safe.

Willie Craig and I try boating across a field at La Paloma Ranch north of Santa Barbara. Photo by Elixabeth Hvolboll.

Viva la Fiesta!

Norbert Schiller loved parades. They embodied his most positive feelings about America. The Santa Barbara Fiesta parade was very different from Nazi marches he had observed with growing horror in his youth in Austria and Germany.

So I would take Norbert to the annual parades, which greatly relieved his wife, Mary, who, though much younger than her husband, had reached the plateau of ennui of many Santa Barbarans regarding the annual conquistadorial tune up.

Norbert just liked all the handsome horses, the cheerleaders in short skirts, the smiling senoritas twirling their ruffles and flashing their white teeth. He loved the excitement of the colorful and raucous crowds packed into aluminum lawn chairs along both sides of State Street, the boys who climbed trees for a balcony view, the business folk watching from upper windows or rooftops. Confetti and candy and music flew through the air.

Taking Norbert to a parade was like taking a four-year-old who would throw 80 years into the gutter along with candy wrappers and popsicle sticks.

We sat on the curb with the candy-catching kids, Norbert's old toes peeking out of aging Birkenstocks. He wore a leather visor over his great head of grey hair, shielding his pale blue eyes from the sun. The candy launchers on the flower-bedecked floats had pretty good aim, mostly missing the old man and cascading sweets among the scrambling children.

And in the midst of this, he managed to shock me.

As the prancing horses and glittering carriages passed by, the crowd called out in a cacophony of mass joy, "Viva la Fiesta! Viva la Fiesta!" Very likely the anticipation of hitting the taco and beer tents after the parade fueled the crowd's reverberation levels.

Norbert suddenly began to chime in with the shouting crowd, "Toutala! Toutala!" he shouted, waving his rumpled handkerchief in the air.

And I turned, suddenly, momentarily, prissy and reprimanded him, "Norbert! Shush! You can't say that! It's embarrassing!"

What he was shouting into the bright sunlight was a word, and other similar words, that he had told me, in moments of intimacy, were old Viennese slang of his youth for the hidden wonders of breasts, sexual intercourse, and a variety of body parts.

Norbert laughed at me. "I celebrate!" he said. "I'm German-Jewish! If anyone in this crowd understands my Vienna words, they will be so happy to remember!"

A little girl in a pink sundress sitting on the other side of Norbert shyly offered him a Tootsie Roll from her bulging pockets.

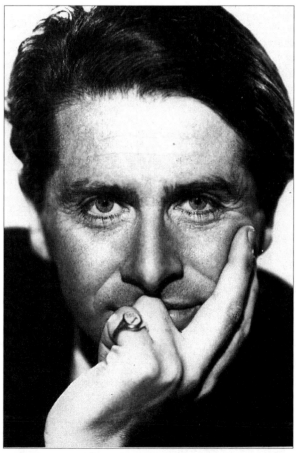

One of Norbert Schiller's promotional photos used when seeking film work in Hollywood probably in the 1940s.

Tears

In the Midwest you rake leaves once a year and revel in it. In Santa Barbara you rake or sweep leaves every day and curse. One guy actually ran for mayor on the single platform of outlawing noisy leaf blowers. And lost. A tall eucalyptus towered over my little flat-roofed house, shedding pink fuzz and knife-blade-shaped gray leaves day after day. There are many small ways you pay for all that nice weather.

I was sweeping up the day's haul from my asphalt driveway when I heard the putt-putt of Willie Craig's old blue Volkswagen van coming down Cliff Drive. He pulled into the driveway, and when the motor died I could hear faint music issuing from the van. Normally Willie would have jumped out and greeted me with a grin and a silly dance, or, as he did one time, and thankfully, just once, when he wasn't wearing his usual suspenders—he sucked in his gut and let his pants fall to his feet amid the Australian ferns by the front door. Hello!

He stayed in the bus. So I ambled over to see what the

matter was, and he was just sitting there, his hands gripping the wheel, great wet tears streaming down his face. "I can't help it," he said. "It happens every time." The car radio's voice sobbed out the dying moments of Madame Butterfly.

Willie loved opera as much as he loved sailing his old 30 ft. fiberglas boat. He spent most of his time in the early 1990s, when I first met him, fussing and fixing the boat, with a local classical station playing accompaniment. He rarely knew what opera he was listening to, but whenever a romantic, tragic Puccini aria was up, the tears would start falling. It was something like a Pavlovian response, a Puccinian.

We started going together to an adult education opera class at the community college, taught by a woman who was not academically trained in music but simply had loved opera all her life, starting with an infatuation with Mario Lanza movies. She was delighted to find that an enthusiastic group of people enjoyed taking her classes as much as she liked giving them. She would talk about the history of an opera, show video segments on screen in the lecture hall, and discuss the details.

Inspired by the class, I bought a few filmed operas, and one of the things Willie and I did on the weekends when he came to stay with me was haul out the opera videos and watch Puccini or Verdi operas. I rather liked Wagner myself, but those videos tended to rapidly produce snores from my companion, so we stuck with the Italians.

And we had our own dramas, ending in deaths as drear as any opera.

Although Willie had been estranged from his ex-wife, son, and daughter for many years, the young man, Billie, had been occasionally coming up from Los Angeles to see Willie, and a pleasant camaraderie was developing. The three of us would have a look at Willie's boat, and father and son would discuss the endless problems of boats and boating, the main thing they had in common. Billie worked as a specialty carpenter, building staircases in new homes sprouting up in Los Angeles basin developments.

From the harbor, we'd head for a pie restaurant for dinner followed by splendiferous pie portions. Billie looked like a younger, taller, straighter version of Willie, his head full of thick curls still blond, whereas Willie's were tending toward the greyer shades. Blue eyes, straight nose, and a wide, wry grin.

And then one day Willie and I were at my house and the phone on the kitchen wall rang. It was a woman's voice, and it was for Willie. Nobody ever called for Willie. He took the phone and listened in silence. He hung up, and fell to the floor. At first he couldn't breathe, and then, as breath returned, the tears began to flow.

I dropped down beside him and put my arms around him. The tears streamed down his freckled cheeks. He was barely able to speak, but he managed to say, "Billie is dead."

I started crying, too, and we both sat there weeping over

the only part of his past that he had tried to hold on to. No music accompanied the tears.

Billie lived in a condo and kept a cute little car he adored in his small garage. Apparently, he had been tinkering with the car late at night, and needed to turn the engine on to test it. He should have opened the garage door, but he didn't. His sister found him on the floor by the car, his tools around him.

The funeral and resulting contacts with ex-wife and daughter caused even more pain as old wounds were opened and slashed. Willie as an angry atheist was dismayed by the family remnant's insistence on religious ceremonies. I was not there, but I know that he was angry, disruptive, and terribly hurt because no one consulted with him about what Billie might have wanted in the way of final rites, the parents in abject opposition. But the mother was paying for it all, so she got her way, and Willie could only feel ever more the outsider.

He returned with an armful of Billie's clothing. That was about all. I am still wearing two pairs of Billie's long-legged light blue jeans, the bottoms of which drag on the ground if I don't turn them up.

And then there was my cat. He had turned up in my backyard several years before I met Willie at a dance. He was a thin gray tabby. He wouldn't come near me. He just sat under my avocado tree and watched me putting tiles into my electric kiln in a makeshift shed behind the house. I did not want a cat, because I knew from experience in Iowa that cats die. So I ignored him for several days. Then I got worried that he might starve, poor thing, and put out a dish of milk. Fatal mistake. Several days passed. No more milk. The cat remained sitting under the tree, regarding me carefully.

When I started firing my kiln in late morning or early afternoon, it wouldn't reach the desired heat and automatically shut off until very late at night. I had learned never to totally trust the automatic shut off. So my alarm clock rang at 2 am one night, and I stumbled to the back door to peek into the shed and check that the little red light had gone off. I trundled right back to bed.

I had no sooner pulled the blanket back over me, when the cat, with a flying pounce, landed directly on the bed beside me. And purred. I had been chosen. Next morning I bought cat food, and Persistent settled in. He was an indoor and outdoor cat, but he was always there at night to sleep cuddled up next to me.

That is, until Willie danced into our lives, and took up the cat's place beside me in bed on the weekends that he came to stay. He loved the cat as I did, but his physical presence displaced Persistent to the foot of the bed.

I think that if there are guardian angels, sometimes they come in cat bodies. It makes no rational sense, but I always felt that once Willie arrived in my life, the cat knew that he could now move on to befriend another loner, and he developed renal failure and died. During that last painful week of his life, I slept on the carpet beside him, saying my farewells with my hands and my tears. And then he was gone, his thin body stilled.

Willie walked in an hour later, and when he saw me on the floor with the cat, crying, he knelt beside me, and the tears flowed from his eyes as well. It was a totally Puccini time. Just without the music.

Willie dug a burial pit in the sandy backyard, and we wrapped Persistent in towels and placed his body softly in the grave. I set a large painted tile of a cat over the spot, and the two of us stood there weeping. Happily, California backyards are fenced, so the neighbors don't often get to observe the dramas.

One weekend morning Willie sailed his old boat, Swing Dancer, up the coast from Ventura to Santa Barbara, instead of driving up the coast highway in his rattley VW van. I picked him up at the harbor. "Come with me tonight back to Ventura," he coaxed.

I had a few business excuses, but none of them that evening ranked with the idea of a pleasant cruise down the coastline thirty miles. "The weather's nice," he said, as we headed for my car. "There's a bit of a breeze so we can sail instead of running the diesel. And," this was the clincher, "there's a big bag of peanut M&Ms on board."

We drove my VW bug down to the harbor, just as the sun was going down. "We might even get a sunset tonight," Willie grinned, pushing his Greek fisherman's cap back and studying the gathering clouds. Sunsets were much rarer in California than in the Midwest, so any offering of red skies at sunset were happily observed. Willie's light blue boat, tied up at a visitors' wharf, was shifting gently from side to side, as if it were anxious to pull loose and run.

He looked at his watch. "Okay, let's get moving," he said, his blue eyes smiling. He helped me onto the boat, untied his lines, hopped on board, and, under the little diesel motor's power, we slowly turned around and headed out of the harbor into the open sea.

Once we were past the entanglements of seaweed and in safely deep water, he turned us toward the south and maintained that safe distance from shore. We could see clusters of lights beginning to sparkle in the darkening shadows of the city and the foothills beyond.

The sun was now long in bed, and a full moon had taken its place. It appeared determined to float across the sky, even though hampered by dense striations of dark clouds. Whenever the round globe emerged, the clouds around it would be edged in soft silvery light. We watched the moon playing hide and seek, and we stretched our arms out to the warm night air and the light breeze that now pushed our sails along. The diesel motor was stilled. Willie and I stood, our arms around each other, listening to the delicate plop and whoosh of water against the bow, amid the silence of the ocean at night.

Willie looked at his watch.

"I can't believe you're worried about what time it is," I laughed. He grinned at me, raised an eyebrow and one finger, and jumped down the hatch to the little galley area below.

Suddenly the night sky was filled with a soaring voice, a thrilling, world encompassing energy of song that was Pavarotti. Nessun Dorma.

Willie hopped back up on deck, grinning. "I thought you might like this," he said. "The Three Tenors are singing tonight on radio. I thought they might sing to us."

And sing they did.

We stood on deck listening to their voices fill the universe around us, until we reached the outskirts of Ventura and the beckoning arm of the harbor. Our eyes in the night air were moist.

Willie Craig and me boating across an Iowa junkyard.

In Loving Arms

I LIKE THE SOUND of German words. I like to read them. I didn't learn to speak them any too well the year 1967 that I spent in Hagen-Haspe as an English teaching assistant in a German girls school. But the sound of them got to me. Not the Hitlerian screech or the rasping military commands of the movies, but the everyday coffee sounds, the ecstasy of Schubert love songs, and the soft voice of a little blonde girl, maybe three years old, who walked up to me, hung her head, and peering sidewise, shyly said, "Ich hab' dich lieb, Judith."

She liked me.

Mostly I've learned to read German by simply reading it, without a dictionary, starting with song lyrics and children's books and moving onward to more complex writing. It's the way I learned to read English, too, of course. Eventually, plugging away at this for a number of years after returning from Germany, I climbed up *The Magic Mountain,* or *Der Zauberberg,* by Thomas Mann. I had bought the two paperback volumes in Germany because someone told me the story took place in a TB sanatorium. Since my mother had spent several years in a Norton, Kansas, sanatorium, I was curious.

I encountered a sparkling Milky Way of density, with entwined layers of long words, long sentences, philosophic and descriptive language, and to me it was exceedingly slow going and about eighty percent guesswork. But I was intrigued by the challenge, and soon by what I could decipher about the young man who had traveled to the sanatorium to visit his cousin. He fell in love with a Russian woman who slammed doors and had a beautiful upper arm. I was incapable of skimming, so I dragged through every sentence. The young man didn't even speak to the girl until the end of the first volume, and all he did was ask to borrow her pencil. By the end of the second volume, he never did get the girl, but I sure got a lot of German vocabulary into my head. The word for that in German, *Wortschatz*, means "word treasure." And a treasure it is, though my trunk is mostly full of nouns, adjectives, verbs with hardly a clue, still, as to how the pronouns work. But I can read just about anything these days, nevertheless, and understand most of it.

Right now I am rereading *The Magic Mountain*, and I have to be very careful with it as its leaves are turning brown and falling. Forty years later, the book is a lot easier reading than the first time, and, in parts, funnier than I ever suspected.

There is a folded piece of white paper between the pages,

a bookmark. I moved it several times before I realized there was something written inside it. It was one of Mr. Joseph's favorite poems.

Rudolf Joseph was in his 80s when I met him in Santa Barbara. Because of mutual interests in movies, music, and German poetry, we quickly became friends, and for several years I spent every Wednesday evening with him in his pleasant apartment over a garage. He had been an assistant producer to several prominent theater directors in Berlin when he was very young and very astute. This was in the 1920s and 30s when theater and cabaret in Berlin were the whirling apex of theatrical culture. He was also assistant producer to G.W. Pabst when he was directing Louise Brooks in stylish silent films.

And then, because he was an astute man and could see what was coming, he left Germany as soon as Hitler took power. His parents, although they were part of the cultural upper crust of Frankfort and paid no attention to synagogues, were of Jewish heritage and lost their home.

In the 1950s Mr. Joseph came to Santa Barbara and helped set up the film division for Brooks Institute of Photography. Later he was invited to help found and direct an international film museum for the city of Munich. This he did until he retired and decided to return to Santa Barbara in his 80s. "I was always happy and safe here," he said. "I wanted to come back here for my last years. There was nothing left for me in Germany."

What was most inexorably gone was the actress he had loved for many long years. He had fallen in love with her when she was still married, and, being an honorable man, he waited a very long time until she was free. During his time directing the Munich film museum they were always together, a deep-rooted though late blooming romance. They spent memorable times in Italy. "Those were the best days of my life," he said.

He told me just enough about her to know that she had been the love of his life. He didn't like to talk about it. Her death was still a little too near his heart.

I always took Mr. Joseph to new foreign films in Santa Barbara, walking him and his cane slowly down the stairs and patiently helping to aim his rear end towards the passenger seat of my red VW beetle, without banging his thin white hairs against the arch of the door. Afterward we'd go to a late night restaurant under a huge ficus tree and share an order of cheese-baked potato skins and talk about the movie.

One time we had just settled into our seats at the movie theater and the film was rolling. Mr. Joseph started fumbling for his cane, agitated. "Please," he whispered through his sometimes slippery false teeth, "Please, let's go. I can't be here." We left the theater and in silence drove back to his apartment.

He opened a new bottle of Asti Spumante and poured us both a generous glass. A large sigh of relief issued from his broad, white-shirted breast, and he leaned back in his chair. "I'm sorry," he said, nodding to me. "I hadn't read a review of the film, and I didn't realize it took place in Italy, near where my friend and I spent so many happy hours. I can't bear to look at Italy without her."

It was that night that Mr. Joseph wrote down from memory on a slip of paper the poem by Theodor Sturm that has been in my aging *Magic Mountain* book, volume one, more than twenty years now. Underneath his shaky little pen scratches are my more clearly readable German words in pencil. It begins, "Wer je gelebt in Liebesarmen…" and I will try a translation:

> He who has lived in loving arms
> Can never throughout life be harmed,
> And though he die alone in foreign lands,
> Each moment of each hour he's sipped
> The memory of life upon her lips,
> And death will take him to her hands.

*A photo, now fading, that Willie Craig took on
my parents' 55th wedding anniversary in 1994.*

The Woodland Sign

My father did not intend to be buried in any cemetery. He liked the idea of his iridescent dust settling softly under the pines in the quiet little grove he'd planted on a hill in his fifty-four acres of wooded goat hills a few miles from Guthrie Center, Iowa. Mixed with the ashen memories of my mother.

There was a certain romance in the mixed ashes recipe that probably could be traced directly to Robert Waller's best-selling novel in the early 1990s, *The Bridges of Madison County*. Dad was not a novel reader, but he, along with every other Iowan, read that one. Its boundless success, the millions and millions of dollars it bestowed on its Iowa author, was first-page news in the *Des Moines Register* for weeks on end.

I was still living in Santa Barbara when the book leaped into national consciousness.

A few years before that momentous literary birth, I received a letter from C.J. Niles, a friend in my Audubon,

Iowa, hometown who was trying to conjure a career for herself in advertising and promotion. Enclosed in the letter was the opinion page of the *Des Moines Register,* devoted to the complete transcript of the graduation address of a University of Northern Iowa's dean of business, Robert Waller, to his graduating class. The subject of his address to his business majors was "romance." How to create it and nurture it in your life, as it is more important than money and business. It created a bit of a stir at the *Register* and was followed over the next few months by several more essays from this unusual professor, whose previous writings were mostly dedicated to mathematics theories.

Many people were enthralled with the "romance" speech, myself among them. I wrote to Mr. Waller, who, to my surprise, actually wrote me a letter back. A correspondence quickly developed between the two of us, of which I kept C. J. somewhat informed, since she was responsible for the connection. I had no idea what he looked like or how old he was. But his letters were fascinating.

One of C.J.'s larger clients was an Arabian horse breeder headed for the big time. He was involved with a major Arabian conference somewhere in the Southwest, and C.J. was excited to be paid to attend as a marketing consultant for the firm.

Her voice on the phone was so excited, I had to make her slow down, back up and start over. She was calling me from the Arabian conference. "Judy," she said, nearly out of breath, "You will not believe this. I was walking through the lobby of the conference center and stopped to read a poster with the lectures of the day listed. And right there it said one of the lectures on economics of Arabian horses was by Robert Waller! And it said he was from UNI, so it had to be the same person. So I went over to that lecture room and went in. People were all milling around doing the meet and greet thing. And I picked him out right away. Judy, he looks just like an angel!"

A little later, when he sent me a snapshot of himself in a canoe, I thought he looked more like an old Kansas grandmother with long grey-white hair straggling from under a wide-brimmed sun hat. But another photo of him taken in India displayed a section of tanned, hairless chest in the cleft of the loose white Indian cotton shirt he was wearing, along with a silver necklace and bracelet, a smooth-skinned face with a wide jawline, a sensuous mouth, and large, knowing eyes. With a quick intake of breath and a raising of the eyebrows, I was smitten. As were most women who encountered him. He was androgynous and intriguing. And he was my age, though he seemed older.

Our letters continued. I decided it was high time to meet, during one of my annual summer vacations in Iowa. I knew he was married, so C.J. happily agreed to accompany me on this jaunt of discovery to Cedar Falls. We found his house, a rather small and tenuous looking A-frame house in a wooded and weedy area. As soon as we got there, we realized we probably shouldn't have come. His slim, dark-haired wife, a dancer and potter, was obviously not enthralled with her husband's visiting fans. We also discovered he—they—had an extremely pregnant high school age daughter wearing way too much makeup along with an unpleasant attitude.

Robert was friendly and welcoming, but a little stiff. He was casually dressed in jeans and shirt. We spent the afternoon and evening talking with him. C.J. and I conducted ourselves with an air of businesslike politeness, edged with cautious admiration. He had said we could stay there overnight, but hadn't mentioned that there was no guest room nor guest beds. He showed us where we could sleep on the floor of the living room, which we did. The next morning he appeared in a dusty ochre silk three-piece suit and tie, with a perfectly matching handkerchief in the pocket. He was dressed as the business school dean that day, and he was simply breathtaking.

Letters continued. He had several essays published in the *Des Moines Register,* and so did I.

And then one summer when I planned to be back in Iowa for a week or so, either he or I suggested bringing his wife and his guitar to my family's acreage for an evening cook out and music around a fire, and we'd all stay the night. By now his essays had been published not only by the *Register* but also in a book put out by the Iowa State University press, and he had achieved a modest statewide celebrity status.

My parents loved to have friends come to their wooded hideaway, ones who would enjoy listening to the frogs around the pond and the whipporwills in the darkness of the hickory and oak covered hills. They had much enjoyed Waller's essays and looked forward to meeting him. Mom dusted the windowsills in the little one-room cabin and concocted potato salad while Dad made sure he had plenty of wood for a campfire.

Eventually a pickup lurched slowly up the rutted lane through the trees. To my surprise and secret pleasure, Robert's wife had apparently chosen not to come. We had him all to ourselves.

It was a perfect evening. The frogs sang, the hotdogs sizzled, and after we'd eaten our fill, Robert caressed his guitar and sang his songs to us in his gentle, languid voice. He sang of the high desert plains, of old gamblers in blue suspenders, of wizards and wildness, and the smell of wood smoke in the air. The stars came out and twinkled through the tree canopies encircling us and the sparkling fire.

Finally, my parents yawned audibly, and my dad said, "Well, I think we'll turn in. Fire's about down to ashes. Marge and I'll sleep in the bed in the cabin. . . .You folks want to put your sleeping bags on the floor or . . . ?"

"I'm used to camping under the stars," said Robert. "I'll just put my sleeping bag on the ground near the pond and be perfectly fine."

I seconded the move. I got my sleeping bag from the cabin and Robert retrieved his from his truck. We bid my parents goodnight and slowly walked downhill towards the pond, through the long, soft grasses. The moon hung brightly above the pond, and we settled our sleeping bags in the accommodating grass.

We talked for a long time in a growing intimacy. The word "soulmates" drifted to the surface, and that recognition was sealed with a long, deep, shining kiss. We never, however, left our respective sleeping bags.

Dawn and my father arrived all too soon. He looked mildly amused as he gazed down on us from the rutted driveway. "Marge has coffee on the stove," he said. "That grass looks pretty wet."

The wet blankets calmed Robert down, but not me. Back in California, I wrote him a couple hot letters. In return he sent me the draft of his next op-ed piece, a celebratory piece about his wife.

That put out the fire in California, but when the Sunday *Des Moines Register* hit the streets, I did have the satisfaction of seeing my evocative essay on the old linotype machine at Audubon's weekly newspaper take the prime front op-ed page position, with appropriate illustrative artwork. And Waller's paean of praise for his wife was relegated to the inside second page. End of that chapter.

Months later, correspondence continuing, somewhat subdued, in one of his letters he wrote about a story idea he'd suddenly thought of on the drive home to Cedar Falls from Red Oak. He was so excited that he headed directly to his computer, and kept on typing for nine days until his arm went numb from carpal tunnel. He thought he'd call it *The Wizard* and show it to the folks at Iowa State.

You can guess the rest.

A few years after *The Bridges of Madison County* phenomenon, Dad felt that he could no longer keep up with the weed cutting at the acreage, and he deeded the property to Guthrie County parks and recreation to preserve it as a wilderness area. They were happy to take on the care of the acreage, and they erected at the entrance gate a handsome brown wooden sign with yellow letters reading Sutcliffe Wilderness Preserve.

I flew to Iowa for the official dedication, and we took Mom from the nursing home so she could be there, too, in the car, for the pleasant speeches and thank you's. She smiled at everyone and looked happy, though she may not have known what was going on.

Afterward Dad asked me to take a picture of him by the new brown and yellow park sign. "This is a lot better than a headstone," he said, leaning his arm on the sign.

"I've wondered though," he mused, "if I shouldn't get some yellow paint and do just a little hand lettering here towards the bottom. Might make it more of an attraction.

"What do you think?," he said. "How about 'Robert Waller Slept Here'?"

Norbert and Mary Schiller at their first home in Ojai, California.

His Castle

MARY SCHILLER made goat cheese sandwiches and sent us off, her 82-year-old husband, Norbert, and me, to Ojai, for the day. Norbert directed my red VW Beetle, into which he had slowly settled his thin and boney self, along the backroads to the village.

Mary had arrived in Ojai as a very young and spiritually ambitious woman. A friend informed her that the two most interesting and unattached males in the entire enlightened area were Krishnamurti and Norbert Schiller.

She sought out Norbert. He was living alone with two goats in the back country in a small, round, stone edifice. He occasionally would go to Los Angeles to play bit parts in movies that needed a handsome, middle-aged face with a German accent, such as Mel Brooks' classic, *Young Franken-stein,* and *Morituri.* He wrote poetry and plays, attempting to form them in English. It was difficult and melancholy. His brightly lit life on the stages of Europe was far away.

Mary was a slim sprite, cheerful, uplifting, and a good

vegetarian cook. She married him. Eventually they moved to Santa Barbara into a normal sort of house with a kitchen and no goats.

Norbert directed the Beetle along narrow roads to his former stone castle, still standing, abandoned but intact, amid arid shrubbery of the California semi-desert. We went inside. Sunlight through a window caressed the shadows.

"See here," he shuffled to a stone and concrete bench extending from the circumference of the inner wall. "This was my bed. The rain in winter on the roof..." He passed his pale hand delicately over the surface of the bench. The roof was still intact.

We sat side by side on the bench and ate our sandwiches. I was beginning to get used to the strange taste of goat in the soft cheese.

"It's been a long time since I've been in Ojai," Norbert said, carefully wiping his silver gray moustache. "Would you mind if we continued on another pilgrimage? There is a woman here whom I used to know and haven't seen for many years. She must be very old now, if she is still alive. She was a true devotee of Krishnamurti."

Norbert sank once again onto the passenger seat in the Beetle, slowly drawing in after him his sandaled feet. He directed our route to his friend's house, and the gravel roads became narrower and sandier the further we went.

Finally we reached a little gray wooden house under tall, gray-green, overhanging valley oaks. Surprisingly, another car had arrived prior to ours. A social services woman stood on the little front porch brushing the long white hair of a very old woman seated on a wooden chair. She was small, slim, wearing a modest and unrevealing cotton gown.

"Norbert," I whispered. "I think I will look like that when I'm her age."

The social services woman tapped the long haired wraith on the shoulder, and she turned and saw us, but not clearly. The helpful woman waved to us, "Wait just a little while, until I'm finished, then I'll put her back in bed, and you can visit her then. She'll be happy to have a visitor."

We walked around the perimeter of the house. One of the rooms was entirely given over to a flock of finches and canaries who fluttered about, twittering, and resting in between flutters on a large, dead branch with many guano-painted twigs. The little bird room was next to her bedroom, separated by a screen, and was apparently her source of music and amusement.

We entered the house and Norbert, who knew his way around it, took me into a small room, quite clean, with photos of Krishnamurti on the wooden walls and a small shrine to him on a table. She had kept his memory beloved within her home.

The social worker came to us, said she was "taking off now," and that Norbert's friend was in her bed, waiting.

Norbert, his back a little bowed, his gray hair standing up in lively peaks, shuffled into the room. She was lying in the middle of a high bedstead, covers pulled up around her white nightgown, her hair braided and coiled neatly around her head. He spoke to her, but, smiling, she gestured that she was hard of hearing. He moved around to the far side of the bed—I was standing quietly in the doorway, more or less invisible to these two—and he awkwardly but purposefully climbed onto the bed and lay down beside her, his mouth and moustache close to her ear.

I slipped softly back to Krishnamurti, leaving the two old friends to communicate as best they might, both of them knowing it would be their last conversation.

After a little while, Norbert came to me and motioned that it was time to go. We walked to the car in silence. I helped him slump into his seat.

There was nothing to say, so we said nothing until we reached the outskirts of Santa Barbara.

A Little Love Story

SOME PEOPLE COLLECT salt and pepper shakers; some collect Dead Sopranos.

I've known a few in the latter category, devotees of Callas, Supervia, Olivera, Flagstad, or — most especially — Lotte Lehmann, born in Germany in 1888, famous from the early 1900s to her retirement from opera and lieder in the 1960s. She died in 1976 in the home in Santa Barbara she shared with her companion, Frances Holden. And I was friends with Frances, born in 1900, for several years dating from 1987.

Dead Soprano collectors may amass vast collections of old 78 rpm recordings of their most revered voices. They may studiously compile discographic listings of every recording the beloved ever made, noting the numbers, the variants, even the pitch at which the recordings were made. Yet none of the Lehmann collectors I knew ever confused the technicalities with the heart and soul of the singer.

The collector I knew best was Gary Hickling, a contemporary. He is a classical bass viol musician living in Hawaii who had happened during his college years to meet Lotte Lehmann in Santa Barbara, and, like many men over many years, he fell totally under the spell of the voice and the woman. This resulted, by 1987, in a very detailed discography of Lehmann's recordings.

"Whenever she wanted a new hat, she'd run in to the studio and whip out a recording," said Gary. " She was very, very good at studio recording."

The Santa Barbara university library's special collections unit in 1987 was planning a centennial celebration of Lehmann's birth for 1988. A biography was in the works, and Gary surfaced with his discography to add to the book. That's when I met him.

Gary and I hit it off, and, after the centennial, decided to start a "zine" called The Lotte Lehmann League. We wrote articles about Lehmann and her recordings, printed up little booklets and sent them out to a small mailing list of aficionados.

A perfectionist, Gary was never quite satisfied that he had all the details about all the old Lehmann recordings. So he suggested the two of us go to Germany to track down a few things. I agreed, and off we went.

I knew that Gary would be able to speak German a good deal better than I, but what I didn't realize was how much longer his legs were. Everywhere we went, we walked at a breakneck pace, and every library we went to involved long, steep stairs, which Gary took two at a time, running. I came trotting along behind, puffing, and exercising *sotto voce* the few German swear words I could recall.

One of the people Gary had most looked forward to interviewing was a recording engineer, Horst Wahl, who had worked with Lehmann in Berlin in her vocal prime, between 1925 and 1935. We visited him in Freiburg. He was nearly 90, but sharp and full of energy. He answered Gary's countless technical questions, and we all felt united in love for a voice we considered among the immortal.

Although I couldn't entirely follow all that Horst said, I watched him carefully, and I felt that this man had deeply loved Lehmann, though he didn't precisely say so.

Back in Santa Barbara, I had access to many Lehmann photos, and I sent Horst Wahl a photo of Lehmann in a 1920s-style cloche hat, among others. He wrote back that he was delighted with that photo. It was just as he had remembered Lotte.

Horst had told us in Freiburg that when he was a very young man he worked as a technician for Odeon recording company in the mornings and as a record salesman in the afternoons.

One day a woman in a flapper helmet hat came in and asked to hear some soprano recordings. When asked which singer, she said, "Show me what you think is worth buying." The young Horst Wahl stated categorically, "There is nothing more beautiful than Lotte Lehmann."

She replied, "Thank you, young man," and looked up at him from under her hat, smiling. "That's who I am." The 89-year-old Wahl told us that that was the greatest and most embarrassing moment of his life. After his blushing and stammering were over, he said, he and the soprano talked for hours. His understanding of her voice and of the recording techniques of the day made him one of her very best recording technicians.

That's as far as that story went in the Lotte Lehmann League article on his interview, and in the several biographies that have been written in English and in German about the soprano.

But there is more to the story.

I continued to write to Horst Wahl, in my rather ungrammatical but enthusiastic German, and he continued to write back to me, with charm and warmth. I think, entering his 90s, he wanted someone in the world to know the great love story of his life, a ten-year love affair that he had never revealed to anyone except his wife.

The role most intimately associated with Lehmann is that of the Marschallin in the opera *Der Rosenkavalier*. The Marschallin is a princess in her thirties, wise in the ways of love, who at the beginning of the opera is dallying in her bedroom with a young lover, Octavian, a seventeen-year-old swashbuckler, quickly incensed with youthful jealousy when the Marschallin mentions that she had dreamed of her husband.

This role Lehmann played in real life with the young Horst Wahl. She was 38, he was about 26. I will attempt translating from his letters to me in 1989:

"When Lotte and I met, I was naturally very shy due to the difference in our ages and the fact that she was the greatest soprano of the day. I was simply dying in awe of her. But Lotte very soon took the initiative, as she saw where things stood.

"One day she said to me, 'You love to read Honoré de Balzac. Do you remember this quote from him: What can be sweeter than the love of a ripe woman for a youth, whose first love she is?' That broke the dam...

"Some time later I met her after a Meistersinger performance at the Berlin State Opera (with Michael Bohnen and Wilhelm Furtwangler). She was staying at her hotel (Kaiserhof unter den Linden). It was late at night, and because it was such a lovely summer evening, we decided to walk the short distance. I noticed as we strolled that my Lotte was wearing a new ring that I'd never seen before. Immediately my jealousy awakened. (Not, however, toward her husband, Otto Krause, whose situation I well understood.) And I said to her, 'So what joker now has honored you with this? (My love was frequently put to the test due to Lotte's heavy schedule of celebratory appearances and the necessity for her to be with very famous people.)

"She stopped still under a tall lantern, looked deeply into my eyes, and said, 'My love, you musn't be jealous of this stupid ring. Look at me!' And with the finger upon which the ominous ring glinted, she pointed to the shadows under her eyes. 'These so much sweeter rings—these I have only from you!'"

From another Horst Wahl letter came this remembrance:

"I see her yet today, after more than 60 years, so precisely before me. . . In the hours of our deepest bonding, Lotte one night softly said a poem by Ina Seidel. We called it our sacred place.

"I'm never so near you as in the nights
when darkness vast around us stills;
secretly alive only
your breath rises, your breath falls.

"No other artist have I found who used her breath for erotic expression as did Lotte. Even when she didn't sing a note—her quick, hot, intake of breath just before she began to sing told everything."

Lotte left Germany for the U.S. after refusing to sing for the Third Reich. After her husband died of tuberculosis in New York, Frances Holden became her protective companion, and they moved to Santa Barbara in the 1940s.

In one of the letters, Horst refers to a post-war recording of an American radio interview of Lotte, in German, aimed at German listeners. She talked specifically about her time in Berlin before the war, and at one point, said softly, "I have forgotten nothing."

Later the radio interviewer asked her what recording she would like to end the interview with. She answered, "The Richard Strauss lied *Morgen* would be the recording of my choice."

In German, the word "choice" is "Wahl." And *Morgen* was the favorite recording of Lotte Lehmann and her young engineer Horst Wahl.

I like collecting love stories.

Book designed and typeset by
Judith Sutcliffe. Text type Adobe
Caslon with titles in Tagliente, a
typeface by Judith Sutcliffe:
The Electric Typographer.